THE BATTLE OF ZAMA

Books in the Battles Series:

✦ BATTLES OF THE ANCIENT WORLD ✦

THE BATTLE OF ZAMA

BY DON NARDO

Lucent Books, P.O. Box 289011, San Diego, CA 92198-9011

Library of Congress Cataloging-in-Publication Data

Nardo, Don, 1947-
    The battle of Zama / by Don Nardo.
        p. cm. — (Battles of the ancient world)
    Includes bibliographical references and index.
    ISBN 1-56006-420-X (lib. ed.: alk. paper)
    1. Zama (Extinct city), Battle of, 202 B.C.—Juvenile literature.
2. Punic War, 2nd, 218–201 B.C.—Juvenile literature. 3. Scipio,
Africanus, ca. 236–183 B.C.—Juvenile literature. 4. Hannibal,
247–182 B.C.—Juvenile literature. I. Title. II. Series.
DG247.97.N37 1996
937'.04—dc20   95-11760
                                                                     CIP
                                                                      AC

Contents

Foreword

Almost everyone would agree with William Tecumseh Sherman that war "is all hell." Yet the history of war, and battles in particular, is so fraught with the full spectrum of human emotion and action that it becomes a microcosm of the human experience. Soldiers' lives are condensed and crystallized in a single battle. As Francis Miller explains in his *Photographic History of the Civil War* when describing the war wounded, "It is sudden, the transition from marching bravely at morning on two sound legs, grasping your rifle in two sturdy arms, to lying at nightfall under a tree with a member forever gone."

Decisions made on the battlefield can mean the lives of thousands. A general's pique or indigestion can result in the difference between life and death. Some historians speculate, for example, that Napoleon's fateful defeat at Waterloo was due to the beginnings of stomach cancer. His stomach pain may have been the reason that the normally decisive general was sluggish and reluctant to move his troops. And what kept George McClellan from winning battles during the Civil War? Some scholars and contemporaries believe that it was simple cowardice and fear. Others argue that he felt a gut-wrenching unwillingness to engage in the war of attrition that was characteristic of that particular conflict.

Battle decisions can be magnificently brilliant and horribly costly. At the Battle of Thaspus in 47 B.C., for example, Julius Caesar, facing a numerically superior army, shrewdly ordered his troops onto a narrow strip of land bordering the sea. Just as he expected, his enemy thought he had accidentally trapped himself and divided their forces to surround his troops. By dividing their army, his enemy had given Caesar the strategic edge he needed to defeat them. Other battle orders result in disaster, as in the case of the Battle at Balaklava during the Crimean War in 1854. A British general gave the order to attack a force of withdrawing enemy Russians. But confusion in relaying the order resulted in the 670 men of the Light Brigade's charging in the wrong direction into certain death by heavy enemy cannon fire. Battles are the stuff of history on the grandest scale—their outcomes often determine whether nations are enslaved or liberated.

Moments in battles illustrate the best and worst of human character. In the feeling of terror and the us-versus-them attitude that accompanies war, the enemy can be dehumanized and treated with a contempt that is considered repellent in times of peace. At Wounded Knee, the distrust and anticipation of violence that grew between the Native Americans and American soldiers led to the senseless killing of ninety men, women, and children. And who can forget My Lai, where the deaths of old men, women, and children at the hands of American soldiers shocked an America already disillusioned with the Vietnam War. The murder of six million Jews will remain burned into the human conscience forever as the measure of man's inhumanity to man. These horrors cannot be forgotten. And yet, under the terrible conditions of battle, one can find acts of bravery, kindness, and altruism. During the Battle of Midway, the members of Torpedo Squadron 8, flying in hopelessly antiquated planes and without the benefit of air protection from fighters, tried bravely to fulfill their mission—to destroy the *Kido Butai,* the Japanese Carrier Striking Force. Without air support, the squadron was immediately set upon by Japanese fighters. Nevertheless, each bomber tried valiantly to hit his target. Each failed. Every man but one died in the effort. But by keeping the Japanese fighters busy, the squadron bought time and delayed further Japanese fighter attacks. In the aftermath of the Battle of Isandhlwana in South Africa in 1879, a force of thousands of Zulu warriors trapped a contingent of British troops in a small trading post. After repeated bloody attacks in which many died on both sides, the Zulus, their final victory certain, granted the remaining British their lives as a gesture of respect for their bravery. During World War I, American troops were so touched by the fate of French war orphans that they took up a collection to help them. During the Civil War, soldiers of the North and South would briefly forget that they were enemies and share smokes and coffee across battle lines during the endless nights. These acts seem all the more dramatic, more uplifting, because they indicate that people can continue to behave with humanity when faced with inhumanity.

Lucent Books' Battles Series highlights the vast range of the human character revealed in the ordeal of war. Dramatic narrative describes in exciting and accurate detail the commanders, soldiers, weapons, strategies, and maneuvers involved in each battle. Each volume includes a comprehensive historical context, explaining what brought the parties to war, the events leading to the battle, what factors made the battle important, and the effects it had on the larger war and later events.

The Battles Series also includes a chronology of important dates that gives students an overview, at a glance, of each battle. Sidebars create a broader context by adding enlightening details on leaders, institutions, customs, warships, weapons, and armor mentioned in the narration. Every volume contains numerous maps that allow readers to better visualize troop movements and strategies. In addition, numerous primary and secondary source quotations drawn from both past historical witnesses and modern historians are included. These quotations demonstrate to readers how and where historians derive information about past events. Finally, the volumes in the Battles Series provide a launching point for further reading and research. Each book contains a bibliography designed for student research, as well as a second bibliography that includes the works the author consulted while compiling the book.

Above all, the Battles Series helps illustrate the words of Herodotus, the fifth-century B.C. Greek historian now known as the "father of history." In the opening lines of his great chronicle of the Greek and Persian Wars, the world's first battle book, he set for himself this goal: "To preserve the memory of the past by putting on record the astonishing achievements both of our own and of other peoples; and more particularly, to show how they came into conflict."

Chronology of Events

B.C.

ca. 2000–1000
Latin-speaking tribes descend from central Europe into Italy; the people who later become the Romans build villages on hills near the Tiber River in west-central Italy.

ca. 850
Phoenician traders establish Carthage at the tip of Tunisia in northern Africa.

ca. 800
The Etruscans settle in Etruria in northwestern Italy.

ca. 750
The Latin-speaking villagers unite into a central town called Rome; the Greeks begin colonizing Sicily and southern Italy.

509
The Romans expel their Etruscan king and create a new government called the Roman Republic.

ca. 285
The Romans finish their conquest of central Italy.

280
Pyrrhus, king of the Greek state of Epirus, defends Tarentum and other Italian Greek cities against the Romans in a large battle at Heraclea in southern Italy.

275
Pyrrhus withdraws his army from Italy, leaving the Italian Greeks to face Rome alone.

265
Rome completes its conquest of the Italian Greek cities, becoming master of all Italy south of the Po Valley.

264
Carthage takes control of the strategic Strait of Messina between Italy and Sicily; saying that Carthage is intruding into the Roman sphere of influence, Rome declares war, initiating the First Punic War.

260
The Romans win a decisive naval victory against Carthage near Mylae in northern Sicily.

256
In the largest sea battle fought in ancient times, the Romans defeat the Carthaginian fleet near Sicily's Cape Ecnomus, leaving the northern African coast defenseless.

255
Carthage hires the Greek mercenary general Xanthippus, who defeats the invasion forces of Roman consul Marcus Regulus in a battle fought south of Carthage; over two hundred Roman ships are destroyed in a huge storm off the coast of Sicily.

241
After throwing all its remaining resources into building one last fleet, Rome defeats Carthage in the waters near western Sicily; Carthage begs for peace, ending the First Punic War.

237
Hamilcar begins the conquest of southern Spain in an effort to carve out a Carthaginian kingdom there.

229
Hamilcar dies and his son-in-law Hasdrubal inherits command of Carthaginian Spain; the Romans send forces into Illyria, across the Adriatic Sea from eastern Italy.

225–220
Rome defeats the Gauls in the Po Valley, expanding its power over all Italian lands south of the Alps.

221
Hasdrubal is murdered and succeeded by Hannibal, Hamilcar's son.

220–219
Hannibal besieges and captures Saguntum, Rome's ally on the eastern Spanish coast.

218

Rome demands that Carthage surrender Hannibal and when Carthage refuses, the Romans declare war, initiating the Second Punic War; Hannibal crosses the Alps into Italy and defeats the Romans at the Trebia River.

217

Hannibal defeats the Romans at Lake Trasimene, north of Rome; the Romans appoint a dictator, Fabius Maximus, to deal with the emergency.

216

In a major battle fought near Cannae, in southeastern Italy, Hannibal hands Rome the worst single military defeat in its history.

215

Hannibal makes an alliance with King Philip V of Macedonia, who promises to invade Italy.

211

The Romans recapture Capua, on the western Italian coast, which had defected to Hannibal, and also Saguntum in Spain.

208–207

Hannibal's brother, Hasdrubal Barca, leads an army from Spain, over the Alps, and into northern Italy; soon afterward, the Romans decisively defeat Hasdrubal near the Metaurus River.

205

Publius Cornelius Scipio the Younger establishes a base in Sicily in preparation for invading Africa.

204

Scipio invades northern Africa and lays siege to Utica, about twenty-five miles from Carthage.

203

Hannibal abandons Italy and lands his army in northern Africa.

202

On the Plain of Zama, southwest of Carthage, Scipio defeats Hannibal, ending the war; the peace treaty forces Carthage to give up most of its Mediterranean possessions, burn most of its warships, and pay Rome a huge annual war indemnity.

200–197

Rome conquers Macedonia, achieving vengeance against King Philip for helping Hannibal.

193

Hannibal and Scipio meet and converse in the court of the Seleucid king Antiochus III.

190

Rome defeats the Seleucid kingdom.

183

Having been outlawed by his own country, Hannibal commits suicide while in exile.

154

The Numidians, led by Masinissa, fight Carthage for possession of disputed territory in northern Africa.

149

Claiming that Carthage's fight with Masinissa violates the peace treaty ending the Roman-Carthaginian conflict, Rome declares war, starting the Third Punic War; the Romans invade Africa.

147

Scipio Aemilianus, adopted grandson of the Scipio who beat Hannibal at Zama, assumes command of Rome's forces and besieges Carthage.

146

The Romans capture and burn Carthage, then raze the city completely, forever eliminating most aspects of the Carthaginian culture.

INTRODUCTION

The World to the Victor

On a spring morning in the year 202 B.C., two armies faced each other silently on the dusty plain known as Zama, in northern Africa. On one side, massed in three long lines, one behind the other, were the forces commanded by Hannibal, the great Carthaginian general. Some of these men were, like Hannibal, natives of the prosperous city of Carthage, located about seventy-five miles northward on the coast of the Mediterranean Sea. They had come here to fight for their city, their country, and their very way of life. Hannibal's other men were mercenaries, hired foreign soldiers, who fought mainly for money and glory.

On the opposing side, also massed in three ranks, were the Romans, staring grimly from behind their four-foot-long, rectangular shields. Led by the best Roman general of the day, Publius Cornelius Scipio, they had journeyed the 350 miles from their homeland in Italy to put an end to a war that had already lasted almost seventeen years and wiped out nearly an entire generation of Roman men. During this second great conflict between Rome and Carthage, Hannibal had ravaged Italy, defeating every army the desperate Romans had thrown against him. Now, Rome had brought the war to the enemy's homeland, determined to make Hannibal and his soldiers pay in blood.

As he rode up and down the Roman ranks, encouraging his men, Scipio reminded them of the Carthaginians' past crimes against Rome. According to the ancient Roman historian Appian, Scipio, "in the sight of his army, invoked [called upon] the gods, whom the Carthaginians had offended every time they violated

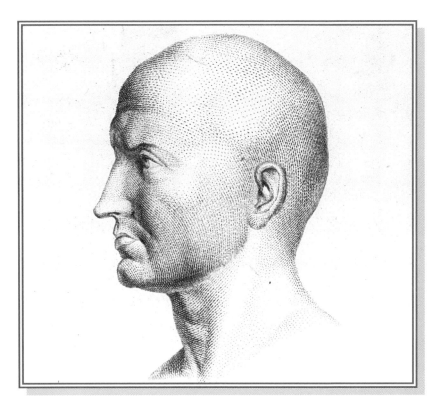

Publius Cornelius Scipio, later called Scipio Africanus, led the Romans in the struggle at Zama.

the treaties [previously made between the two peoples]." At the same time, Hannibal delivered his own enthusiastic battle speech. He "reminded his men of what they had done in Italy, and of their great and brilliant victories won . . . over armies composed entirely of Italians." Fully exploiting the great personal magnetism for which he was famous, Hannibal said that the coming battle "would decide the fate of Carthage and all Africa. If vanquished, they would be enslaved."

But on that day at Zama much more was at stake than the immediate fate of the Carthaginian soldiers and their city. Rome and Carthage were the two most powerful nations in the Mediterranean region, at the time the most populous and culturally developed area in the world. The winner of the Second Punic War would be able to dominate the region, both politically and economically, perhaps for many generations to come. Much was riding, therefore, on the outcome of this last great military encounter of the war. "Is there anyone who can remain unmoved in reading the narrative of such an encounter?" asked the Greek/Roman historian Polybius.

> For it would be impossible to find more valiant soldiers, or generals who had been more successful and were more thoroughly exercised in the art of war, nor indeed had Fortune

Hannibal (left foreground) and Scipio meet shortly before the opening of the massive and fateful Zama battle.

ever offered to contending armies a more splendid prize of victory, since the conquerors would not be the masters of Africa and Europe alone, but of all those parts of the world which now hold a place in history.

At the time, Polybius could not have foreseen that the outcome of the war would have effects reaching far beyond his own day. The victor would, over the course of many centuries, develop the largest empire the world had ever seen. This empire's laws, language, religion, and social customs would profoundly affect the development of the European, or Western, nations that eventually grew in its place. In this way, the outcome of a war fought in the third century B.C. would indirectly influence the course of modern as well as ancient history. "For the West, therefore," comments classical historian Michael Grant, "with the possible exception of the struggles of the twentieth century A.D., the Second Punic War proved to have been the most momentous war of all time."

But it is unlikely that the common soldiers facing each other at Zama pondered the fates of empires and nations to come. All that mattered at that moment was following orders, fighting hard, and surviving the coming struggle. Like all soldiers before and after them, they would do their duty and entrust the work of empire building to the kings and politicians. To the Roman and Carthaginian troops, that duty was to stab, impale, and dismember their opponents as skillfully and as brutally as possible. To the winners would come victory and glory. The losers would await sudden death or miserable servitude. This stark choice must have been foremost in the soldiers' minds as they awaited the trumpet blasts signaling the first charge.

CHAPTER ONE

Inevitable Enemies: The Founding of Carthage and Rome

The Battle of Zama in 202 B.C. was the final military engagement of the Second Punic War, a devastating, seventeen-year-long conflict fought between Rome and Carthage. The war was one of three bloody confrontations between the two nations, a mighty death struggle that began in 264 and ended in 146 with the total destruction of one of the warring parties. These were the epic Punic Wars, which forever changed the course of European history. The term "Punic" derives from the Latin word *Punicus*, meaning Phoenician, the name of the Middle Eastern people who founded Carthage in the ninth century B.C.

The main underlying cause of the Punic Wars was the rivalry between Rome and Carthage over domination of the western Mediterranean region. That region is separated from its eastern counterpart by three major landmasses. The first is the "boot" of Italy, which juts down some five hundred miles from southern Europe into the sea. The second is the island of Sicily, lying just west of the toe of the Italian boot. And the third is Africa's Tunisian peninsula, which protrudes northward, separated from Sicily by a stretch of open sea less than a hundred miles wide. This stretch and the narrow Strait of Messina between Sicily and Italy are the only sea routes connecting the western and eastern Mediterranean regions.

It is not difficult to see why both Carthage, located near the northern tip of the broad Tunisian peninsula, and Rome, situated on the Tiber River fifteen miles inland from the western Italian coast, sought to control the western region. The area encompassed not only Italy, Sicily, and northern Africa, but also southern

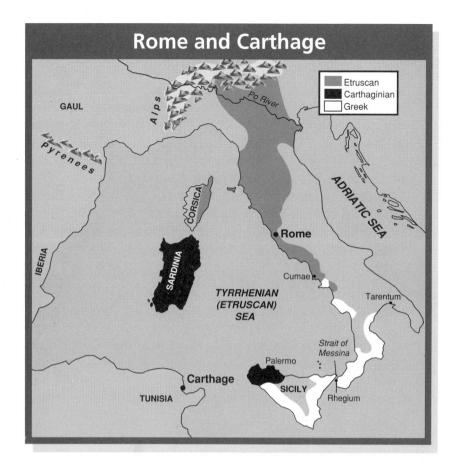

Rome and Carthage

Legend:
- Etruscan
- Carthaginian
- Greek

GAUL

Alps

Po River

Pyrenees

CORSICA

IBERIA

SARDINIA

ADRIATIC SEA

Rome

Cumae

Tarentum

TYRRHENIAN (ETRUSCAN) SEA

Strait of Messina

Palermo

Carthage

SICILY

TUNISIA

Rhegium

France (then called Gaul), Spain (then known as Iberia), and Sardinia and Corsica, the large islands lying directly west of Italy. All these lands possessed fertile plains, expansive forests, and abundant minerals, as well as game, fish, and other natural resources. Dominating the region and its valuable network of trade routes would make any nation wealthy and powerful.

Competing for the Western Sea

In fact, the Romans and Carthaginians were not the first peoples to vie for control of the western trade routes. Centuries before the Punic Wars, when Rome and Carthage were small towns possessing little power and influence, the region was dominated by the Etruscans and the Greeks. The original home of the Etruscans is not known for certain but was probably in Asia Minor, what is now Turkey, in the eastern Mediterranean. Some time around 800 B.C., bands of Etruscans settled in the fertile Italian region north of Rome. Both the ancient and modern names for the area—Etruria and Tuscany—came from the name of the inhabitants. The Etruscans were highly skilled craftspeople who became known for their fine pottery and gold and bronze artifacts. They were also the most organized and influential people to sail the western sea at the time, and they quickly dominated the local trade routes. According to historian James Henry Breasted:

> The leading Etruscans became industrial and commercial princes who did not give up the seafaring life. The triangular basin enclosed by Italy and the three islands—Corsica, Sardinia, and Sicily—finally came to be called the Tyrrhenian, that is, the Etruscan, Sea. From these waters the Etruscans marketed their wares far and wide throughout the Mediterranean. At the same time they also carried on trade with the north through the passes of the Alps [on Italy's northern border]. They lived in walled towns, and each town was the home of a powerful Etruscan merchant-lord, who with his wealthy kindred formed the aristocracy which governed the town.

In time, the Etruscans found themselves in a growing competition with two other eastern peoples who found the western Mediterranean region attractive for trade and settlement. These were the Greeks and the Phoenicians. The Greek settlers came from large cities such as Athens, in eastern Greece, and Miletus, on the western coast of Asia Minor. In the 700s and 600s B.C. they established many towns in Sicily, southern Italy, and the coasts of Gaul and Spain. The Phoenicians, whose homeland was in what

Shards from an Etruscan vase depict a mythical hero. Etruscan artisans produced fine pottery, as well as gold jewelry and other metal artifacts.

Reminders of a Vanished Civilization

The Etruscans were the first people to successfully exploit the western Mediterranean seaways, over which the Romans and Carthaginians would later fight. The major basis of the Etruscans' wealth and trading network was their skill in working with various metals, including gold, silver, copper, tin, and iron. Etruria was the only area of Italy that was naturally rich in metal ores, and the people exploited this advantage to the best of their ability. Etruscan goldsmiths turned out some of the most beautiful gold jewelry and artifacts made in the ancient Mediterranean region. Although they found some of their gold locally, large portions no doubt came from ore-hunting expeditions into the Po Valley and perhaps even beyond the Alps.

The Etruscans also worked extensively with copper and tin, which they combined to produce the stronger and more durable alloy known as bronze. Archaeologists have found a number of bronze swords, daggers, cups, and plates made by Etruscan metalworkers. In time, as the ores of the even more durable iron were discovered, these workers largely abandoned copper and bronze and produced mainly iron artifacts. Their supplies of iron ore came from as far as Spain, northern France, and possibly even Britain. So many Etruscan iron furnaces operated in Etruria's Populonia region that visitors walking in that area of northern Italy today frequently find pieces of iron slag, the unused by-product of the iron-working process. These artifacts constitute silent but potent reminders of a prosperous civilization long since vanished.

is now Lebanon at the far eastern edge of the Mediterranean, were hardy sailors, explorers, and merchants. From the ninth to the seventh centuries, they founded small trading posts and colonies throughout the western sea. These included locations in Sicily, Sardinia, Corsica, Spain, and northern Africa. The Phoenicians eventually controlled nearly all the trade between Sicily and the nearby African coast. Not surprisingly, the rivalry among the western sea's major powers was intense, and the competition between the Greeks and Phoenicians became especially fierce. As archaeologist and historian Leonard Cottrell explains:

> For four centuries there was a bitter struggle for control of the coasts and islands of the west Mediterranean, and battle after battle was fought in the seas around Sicily, between the Phoenicians, who wanted to preserve their monopoly of trade in these regions, and the Greeks, who were equally determined to secure their share. It was one of the bitterest of trade wars in which the descendants of the Phoenicians more than held their own, under the leadership of their most powerful colony, Carthage.

Phoenician merchants hawk their wares and strike deals in the busy outdoor marketplace of a Mediterranean port city.

Living for Trade

Carthage, which emerged by about 500 B.C. as a major western Mediterranean power, had begun as a humble Phoenician trading post on the Tunisian coast. According to a well-known legend, a Phoenician princess named Dido established Carthage some time in the mid-ninth century. Supposedly, Dido fled from Tyre, the chief city in the Phoenician homeland, to escape the cruelty of her brother, the king's son. Landing in the inlet that later became Carthage's magnificent harbor, she bargained with the local people for a piece of land on which to build a town. The legend cannot be verified, but there is no doubt that by 800 or so Carthage was well established as a small but busy Phoenician trading post.

But Carthage did not remain a mere trading post for long. Over the course of several centuries, it advanced to city-state status and took control of numerous other Phoenician outposts in the western sea and established several new ones. In time, continued and expanding trade transformed Carthage, along with its surrounding territory and numerous outposts and allies, into a prosperous and wealthy empire. "The rule of Carthage over this empire was a harsh and exacting one," writes classical scholar Dorothy Mills. Indeed, the early Carthaginian kings cared about little but the inflow of money that ensured their own comforts and the splendor of the mother city. Of the common people, those who worked hard to support the mercantile establishment led decent lives, while those who did not were severely punished. Carthage, Mills continues, "had little genius for law and order and none of the qualities which would have fitted her to become the ruler of men. She lived for trade, and believing there was nothing that money could not buy, was willing to sacrifice everything for her love of gain."

The structure of Carthage's government reflected this money-based philosophy. At first, the city-state, like most other ancient realms, was ruled by kings. But as the leaders of the merchant class gained in power and influence, they threw out the kings and established an early form of republic. The government was dominated by a body called the Council of Four Hundred. This group, whose members were all wealthy merchants and traders, held supreme authority over the city and empire. The Council made and enacted laws, punished lawbreakers, and formulated

Dido, the mythical founder of the city of Carthage, uses strips of animal skin to measure the land along the northern Tunisian coast.

both local and foreign policy. To carry out the everyday business of government, the Council appointed two administrators, known as *suffetes*, who had to be very careful not to make mistakes or offend Council members. This was because the Council was very strict and its methods unforgiving. Totally dedicated to maintaining the empire's inflow of wealth, the Council sometimes ordered *suffetes* to be crucified or buried alive for threatening that inflow by committing some relatively minor error. Military generals often suffered similar fates for losing a battle.

However, the Carthaginians believed that a military defeat was not due solely to a commander's blunders. It was also the result of the anger of a god, who expressed wrath by siding with the enemy. The only way to appease an angry god and win back divine favor, the Carthaginians held, was to offer sacrifice. Carthage's gods, including Tanit, Baal, and Melkart, had bestial, or beastlike, as well as human qualities, and they demanded dramatic and severe forms of sacrifice, more often than not the lives

Before the outbreak of the Punic Wars, Carthaginian merchants barter for goods (including a female slave) at the villa of a wealthy Roman.

Carthage's Magnificent Harbors

By the third century B.C., before the onset of the Punic wars, Carthage was a large and impressive city with many fine public buildings and luxurious villas. The city's most famous and imposing feature, however, was the complex of harbors and dock facilities constructed for its mighty navy. In his *Roman History*, the historian Appian recorded this description, taken from eyewitnesses:

> The harbors were so arranged that ships could pass from one to the other. The entrance from the sea was 70 feet wide and could be closed by iron chains. The first harbor, reserved for merchant ships, had a large selection of berths. In the center of the inner harbor was an island, which, like the harbor, was lined with quays [docks], along the whole length of which were boat-houses providing accommodation for 220 ships; above these were lofts for storing the rigging. In front of each boat-house stood two Ionic columns, so that the perimeter of the harbor and of the island looked like a portico [elegant column-lined porch]. On the island itself stood a small building used as a headquarters for the Admiral and as a post for the trumpeters and heralds [messengers]. The island was just opposite the entrance of the harbor and rose steeply from the water, so that while the Admiral could see what was happening outside, little could be seen of the interior of the harbor from the open sea. Even from incoming merchant ships, the arsenals remained hidden, for they were surrounded by a double wall and merchant vessels passed from the first harbor into the town without going through the arsenals.

With an average depth of seven feet and with only thirty-two acres of usable water surface, Carthage's harbors severely restricted movement of the 220 Carthaginian warships. In order to reach the sea, the warships had to traverse the merchant harbor with its clutter of trading vessels.

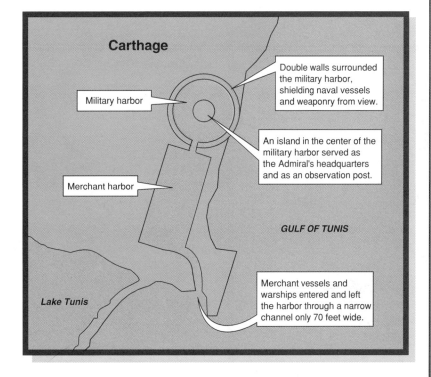

Carthage

Military harbor

Double walls surrounded the military harbor, shielding naval vessels and weaponry from view.

An island in the center of the military harbor served as the Admiral's headquarters and as an observation post.

Merchant harbor

GULF OF TUNIS

Lake Tunis

Merchant vessels and warships entered and left the harbor through a narrow channel only 70 feet wide.

of children. Apparently on a fairly regular basis, children—singly, by the dozens, or even by the hundreds—were thrown into huge ceremonial fires. Such a sacrificial ceremony, report scholars Gilbert and Colette Picard,

> took place at night, by moonlight. In the precinct [sacred area] stood a bronze statue of the god and at his feet a pit was dug in which a fire . . . was lit. Around the statue stood the [priests'] assistants and the parents of the victims, the musicians, and the dancers. A priest would bring the child "dedicated" to the god, already killed according to "secret rites," and lay him in the statue's arms from which he would roll into the flames. Then flutes, tambourines, and lyres [harps] would drown the cries of the parents and lead the dancers into a wild dance.

Most Carthaginians accepted the empire's harsh political and religious practices as commonplace and necessary for maintaining efficiency and prosperity. Therefore, Carthage had a stable government and an overriding religious framework that met most of the needs of the state and the people. Nevertheless, neighboring nations saw Carthaginian society as cruel and its religion as barbaric. As a result, surviving writings from these nations tend to emphasize the negative aspects of Carthaginian culture and minimize the positive features.

Baal, a fertility god of the Phoenicians and later the Carthaginians, was called the "lord of the universe." His religious rituals featured human sacrifice, often of children, and open sexual acts.

An Ancient Art That Survives

According to some archaeological evidence, the ancient Carthaginians, both men and women, may have practiced the art of tattooing, for adornment and also for ritual purposes, that is, to protect the wearer from evil spirits and influences. The Arab Bedouins who inhabit northern Africa today use tattoos, and some experts suggest that several of the more common patterns employed have been handed down through the generations from ancient times. For example, examinations of grotesque masks, perhaps used in Carthaginian religious ceremonies, reveal ornamental patterns that resemble tattoos of common kinds. Describing these masks, the Picards write:

> The forehead is divided by a vertical row of diamond shapes transfixed [pierced] by an arrow pointing towards the nose. The cheeks have horizontal stripes reminiscent of those with which [modern] African blacks and Polynesians decorate their bodies. Others have a single design . . . often a crescent inverted over a disk, the symbol of Tanit and Baal [important Carthaginian gods].

The Resourceful, Aggressive Romans

The Romans, who eventually became the Carthaginians' chief enemies, were especially repulsed by and critical of Carthage and its society. Like Carthage, Rome had humble beginnings. Between 2000 and 1000 B.C., uncultured, nomadic tribes, including groups that spoke an early form of Latin, descended in waves from central Europe into Italy. By the tenth century, the Latin tribes had settled and begun farming in a fertile plain near a bend in the Tiber River, a region they named Latium. Villages grew up in Latium, which was bordered in the east by the rugged Apennine Mountains. In these mountains dwelt fierce hill tribes, descendants of nomads who had entered Italy before the Latins.

About the year 750 a group of neighboring Latin communities united to form a large, although still crude and disorganized, town called Rome. At first, the Romans, rustic and backward farmers, fell under the influence of the more advanced Etruscans who lived just north of Latium. The Etruscans taught the Romans how to build stone buildings, archways, and sewer drains and introduced the counting system that in time came to be known, erroneously, as "Roman" numerals. Eventually, Etruscan kings took charge of Rome and the town flourished. As historian H. H. Scullard comments, "One outstanding aspect of the growth of the city under the Etruscans is its amazing speed: within a century a collection of

A drawing of Rome, made in early modern times depicts some of the ruins of its once imposing structures. A well-preserved triumphal arch rises in the foreground, while the circular shell of the Coliseum looms in the distance.

huts had developed into a city with a civic center [the Forum], public buildings and temples of which the greatest could vie with any in Etruria and indeed in the contemporary Greek world."

Despite the advantages Rome gained from its domination by Etruria, the Romans, a highly resourceful, independent, and aggressive people, were not content to remain under Etruscan rule. In 509 B.C., the Romans expelled their Etruscan king, Tarquinius Superbus, declared his authority null and void, and set up a new government. This was the Roman Republic, under which the city and its territories would thrive and expand for nearly five centuries.

Under the republic, a group of citizens, all free adult males, met periodically in a body known as the Assembly to propose and vote on laws. The Assembly also chose two administrative leaders, the consuls, who were similar to the Carthaginian *suffetes*. The consuls, however, were also the overall military commanders; they held more power and prestige than the *suffetes*, and did not have to fear immediate execution for making mistakes. Though the consuls were popularly elected, the republic was not a democracy. An elite legislative body, the Senate, made up solely of wealthy landowners, held the real power. According to historian R. M. Errington:

> No Roman could achieve political importance without being a member of the Senate. Most senators were ex-magistrates

[high officials]; and all had to pass a scrutiny [close examination] by two censors . . . before they were allowed entry to the Senate. The Senate was therefore a self-perpetuating and exclusive oligarchy [ruling body made up of an elite few], and as a class it tended to close ranks against newcomers.

The senators, nearly all of them heads of Rome's most powerful families, advised the consuls and influenced their policies and, through the granting of money and jobs, controlled how most common citizens voted in the Assembly. Errington continues:

The internal politics of Rome is therefore on the whole not the politics of popular movements led by the chosen leaders of the masses. . . . It is the politics of the governing class, the politics of the Roman Senate. . . . Thus when we say "the Senate decided" or "the Senate thought," what we mean in practice is that a majority of the leaders of the senatorial families decided or thought.

Legislators debate state policy at a session of the early Roman Senate.

The Unification of Italy

In spite of the Senate's dominance, however, over time ordinary Roman citizens gained enough say in government to make them content with the republican system and staunchly proud of it. Therefore, Rome's government proved flexible and popular and, like that of Carthage, largely met the needs of its people. In a similar way, Rome's religion met its people's spiritual needs and helped give the Romans a distinct identity as a national group. The Roman gods, many of them adapted from Etruscan and Greek deities, were not demonic like those of Carthage, but instead, powerful, supernatural versions of human beings. The chief Roman god was Jupiter, whose symbol, the eagle, Rome adopted as its own emblem. Jupiter's wife, Juno, was the goddess of women and childbirth, while Mars was the god of war, Neptune the lord of the sea, and Mercury the overseer of trade and messenger of the gods. The Romans became convinced that these and their other gods favored Rome. It seemed only natural, then, for Rome to attempt to dominate other peoples. Practical, hardworking, and used to hardships, the Romans came to view themselves as having a destiny to exert political, economic, and cultural supremacy over other cities and nations.

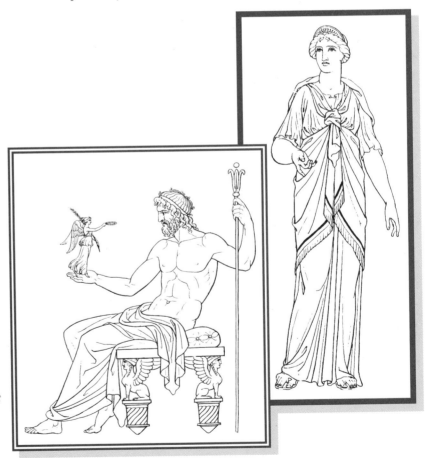

The head Roman god, Jupiter (left), the equivalent of the Greek deity Zeus, sits on his throne. His wife, Juno (right), the counterpart of the Greek goddess Hera, was thought to protect women and to oversee childbirth.

With this superior attitude, beginning in the fifth century B.C., the Romans expanded outward from Latium and subdued their neighbors. During more than two centuries of nearly constant local wars, many of them long and bloody, Rome overcame and absorbed its onetime ruler, Etruria, and went on to conquer dozens of Italian hill tribes. These included the fierce Samnites of south-central Italy, as well as the Volsci, Aequi, and Sabines, who spoke Oscan, a language distantly related to Latin. By 285, Rome controlled all of central Italy. The Po Valley in the north, directly south of the Alps, remained in the hands of the Gauls (or Celts), a rustic, hardy, tribal people. And southern Italy was still the domain of dozens of Greek cities, the largest and richest being Tarentum, at the heel of the Italian boot.

The Romans gazed on these Greek cities with envious eyes. At the time, Tarentum was larger than Rome and had the biggest fleet in Italy. Many of the larger Greek communities were wealthier than Rome, and all were more culturally advanced, possessing magnificent temples and public buildings, as well as artistic and literary traditions that Rome lacked. Rome, however, was superior to these cities in military strength. Relying on this advantage, in 282 Rome made threatening moves on Tarentum. Realizing that they were no match for Rome, the Tarentines and their neighbors appealed for aid from the fellow Greek state of Epirus. Located across the narrow Adriatic Sea, which separates Italy from extreme northwestern Greece, Epirus was ruled by a king named Pyrrhus. He had a formidable army and a reputation as a military general to match. As Michael Grant explains:

The Greek general Pyrrhus, king of Epirus, who narrowly defeated the Romans or fought them to a draw on several occasions.

Pyrrhus, who claimed descent from Alexander the Great [the Greek general who had carved out an empire stretching from Greece to India in the preceding century], was one of the foremost of the minor rulers and rent-an-army generals who had proliferated [grown in number] since Alexander's death a half century earlier. Accepting the invitation from Tarentum, he proclaimed that he would put an end to the Roman power threatening the liberty of the western Greeks. Then he set sail for south Italy, taking with him twenty-five thousand mercenaries, the most highly esteemed professional soldiers of their day, many of them veterans of extensive military experience. And so the Romans had to prepare for the first battles they had ever fought against a Greek army and a Greek state.

Greek Versus Roman Military Systems

Pyrrhus's main offensive device was the Macedonian phalanx, which many nations and almost all mercenaries used at the time. This unique battle formation consisted of thousands of soldiers standing in ranks, one behind the other, each man wielding a spear. The men in each succeeding rear rank held increasingly longer spears, so that the tips all protruded from the front of the phalanx. With this massive frontal array of metal spear points, the phalanx resembled a giant porcupine with its quills erect. When the mighty and seemingly impenetrable formation moved forward, it was frightening and nearly unstoppable.

By contrast, the Romans did not employ the phalanx. Early Roman armies consisted of legions, which were groups of about forty-five hundred soldiers. Each legion had its own commander, who reported directly to one or both of the consuls. A typical legion consisted of about ten subdivisions called cohorts, and each cohort was composed of several maniples, or groups of 60 to 120 men. Roman battle tactics called for cohorts and maniples to march into battle in small separate groups that formed strategic patterns. For example, sometimes the maniples were arranged in a checkerboard fashion. Each individual group was much less

The front ranks of the massive and deadly Macedonian phalanx, with its impenetrable barrier of shields and pikes, mow down the soldiers of an opposing army.

In this sculpted carving, Roman legionnaires mass their shields together to provide a wall of protection against enemy arrows, spears, and other missiles.

formidable than a Greek phalanx. Yet the Roman units could move back, forward, and around quickly at a general's command, giving the Roman army a degree of flexibility that the monolithic phalanx lacked. Both the Romans and the Greeks also employed cavalry, or mounted soldiers, whose task was to outflank, or ride around and behind, the enemy ranks.

The first confrontation between Pyrrhus and the Romans, near Heraclea in southern Italy in 280 B.C., shaped up as a test of two fighting systems—the Greek and the Roman. But the test proved inconclusive, for Pyrrhus brought about twenty Indian elephants into the battle. Unprepared and frightened, the Roman horses, along with many of their riders, panicked. According to the Roman historian Lucius Florus in his *Epitome* [brief account] *of Roman History*, the elephants, "turned the battle into a wild-beast show; for the horses, frightened by their huge bulk and ugliness and also by their strange smell and trumpeting, imagining the unfamiliar monsters to be more formidable than they really were, caused panic and destruction far and wide."

Romans and Pyrrhus's forces, which include several elephants, engage in battle. At first, the Roman troops were terrified of these beasts.

Pyrrhus Defends the Italian Greeks Against Rome

ITALY

Heraclea • • Tarentum

Epirus

GREECE

SICILY

Athens •

280 B.C., Pyrrhus defeats Romans at Heraclea, but sustains heavy losses.

Thanks to the elephants, Pyrrhus won this first battle, but the Romans, who were skilled and stubborn fighters, still managed to inflict significant losses on the Greeks. Most of the encounters between these opponents in the next few years had similar results, and the war remained largely indecisive. Finally, in 275, Pyrrhus decided that defeating Rome was too costly and returned to Epirus. Abandoned to face Rome alone, the Italian Greeks had little choice but submission, and by 265 Rome had gained control of all of Italy with the exception of the Po valley in the north.

A Brave Field of War

The Romans had managed to conquer and absorb the Etruscans and Greeks, two of the main competitors for control of the western Mediterranean. Eager to gain that control, Rome, now a world power, set its sights outward beyond Italy. As Lucius Florus put it, "Italy having been subdued and conquered, the Roman people, having almost reached [their] five hundredth year . . . [were] now robust and vigorous . . . and became a match for the whole world." The first stepping-stone beyond Italy was Sicily, only a few miles across the Strait of Messina. The island, large and rich in forests, fisheries, minerals, and other natural resources, was a tempting prize. According to Florus:

The Romans, victorious over Italy, having now extended their bounds to the Strait [of Messina], halted for a space, like a fire, which, having laid waste the woods that lie in its course, is held up by an intervening river. But soon, seeing in their neighborhood a most wealthy prey [Sicily] . . . they were kindled with so strong a desire for its possession that . . . they resolved that it should be reunited [to Italy] by arms and warfare, and thus restored to the continent to which it belonged.

But it soon became clear that acquiring Sicily would not be an easy undertaking. The eastern part of the island, including the strategic Messina waterway, was controlled by several Greek cities, led by powerful Syracuse. And the remainder of Sicily was dominated by a much more formidable foe—Carthage. Over the centuries during which the Roman Republic had methodically conquered Italy, the Carthaginian empire had spread over most of the western Mediterranean's shores and islands. Carthage's fleets, both commercial and military, were the largest and most powerful in the world. Thus, in a region where once many small and medium-sized powers had vied for shares of the wealth, two superpowers—Rome and Carthage—had emerged and now warily faced each other.

The advantages and disadvantages possessed by each side were obvious to all concerned. Carthage, with a population of one to two hundred thousand, was a magnificent city, three times larger than Rome and much wealthier. It had impressive stone public buildings and two beautiful harbors with modern docks and facilities for over two hundred ships. The Carthaginian empire, including towns and ports in Sicily, Corsica, Sardinia, southern Gaul, and Numidia, the region of northern Africa west of Carthage, encompassed at least 1.5 million people.

In contrast, Rome, with fifty to seventy-five thousand inhabitants, was a shabby, dirty city with few modern stone buildings. The Romans had no war fleets and no trained admirals and sailors to match those of Carthage. And the human resources of Rome and its recently conquered Italian subject peoples totaled no more than a million souls.

Yet the Romans had an important resource that Carthage lacked—a strong, highly trained land army composed of citizen-soldiers. At the time, most Roman troops were farmers and other landowners who, when called on by the state, fought for their nation, homes, and families. Their loyalty and willingness to stick out a tough campaign, combined with their excellent weapons and training, made the Roman army equal to the best in the Mediterranean world. That Rome had fought Pyrrhus's mighty phalanxes to a draw was ample proof of this.

Carthaginian armies, on the other hand, consisted almost exclusively of mercenaries. Although they regularly employed the effective Greek phalanx, these paid fighters usually cared little for the city or nation that hired them and therefore could not always be counted on to give their all. And mercenary generals, who varied widely in training, skills, and experience, could be as unreliable as their men. Thus Carthage, though superior on the seas, could not equal the Romans on land. As a result, in the 260s B.C. the two opponents—one strong on land, the other at sea—were about evenly matched militarily.

It seemed inevitable at the time that the two powers would become enemies and challenge each other for control of the western Mediterranean. "Both nations," remarked Florus, "at the same time with equally strong desires and equal forces were aiming at the empire of the world." Pyrrhus had wisely foreseen the coming struggle and said as he returned to Epirus, "How brave a field of war do we leave, my friends, for the Romans and Carthaginians to fight in." What neither Pyrrhus nor anyone else at the time foresaw was the gigantic scope, terrible brutality, and horrendous loss of life of the Roman-Carthaginian conflicts to come. Unaware that they were about to launch the most destructive war humanity had yet experienced, both sides were eager to prove themselves superior. All they needed was a reason to initiate hostilities and, as if on cue, the residents of Sicily suddenly provided that reason.

CHAPTER TWO

Blood in the Waters: The Fight for Naval Supremacy

To the leaders of Rome and Carthage, war seemed to be the only logical and practical means of obtaining the same long-term goal: control of the western Mediterranean. Neither side expected the other voluntarily to relinquish its share of territory and influence in the region. So the idea of bargaining peacefully for possessions and power never came up. A few brief negotiations between the parties had occurred in the past. In the sixth century B.C., for instance, each had agreed to stay out of the other's sphere of influence—this meant Italy for Rome and the western seas and islands for Carthage. The nations had renewed this agreement in 348 and again in 279. But as the third century B.C. drew to a close, it was clear to both sides that their respective spheres could not remain separate forever. There was little doubt that each desired dominion over the other and that sooner or later armed conflict would result.

It is clear that in preparing for the coming struggle, each side seriously underestimated the other's abilities, resources, and resolve. At the same time, both badly misjudged how difficult and bloody such a war would be. This was illustrated in the way both Rome and Carthage approached the initial goal—seizure and control of the Strait of Messina. For Rome, achievement of this goal would ensure that its merchant ships, many of them recently acquired from the defeated Greek cities, could pass freely between the western and eastern Italian coasts. It would also give the Romans an inroad into Sicily, which they hoped eventually to absorb. For Carthage, control of the strait would ease the tasks of maintaining its monopoly of western sea trade and exploiting

The Strait of Messina

Sicily's resources. Apparently, each side believed that victory in a conflict over the strait and Sicily would be fairly quick and easy. This would prove to be a grave misjudgment, and both Rome and Carthage would pay dearly for their arrogance.

The Death Struggle Begins

The anticipated outbreak of hostilities between the western Mediterranean's superpowers occurred shortly after Rome's successful conquest of Greek-controlled southern Italy. In 265 B.C., the powerful Greek Sicilian city of Syracuse launched an attack on the city of Messina, located in northeastern Sicily along the strategic strait. The Syracusans wanted to wipe out a band of pirates who had seized Messina a few years before and had been terrorizing eastern Sicily ever since. The besieged pirates split into two factions and, as Polybius recorded,

> some of them appealed to the Carthaginians, proposing to put themselves and the citadel [Messina's main fortress] into their hands, while others sent an embassy to Rome, offering to surrender the city and begging for assistance as a kindred people. . . . The Romans, foreseeing [a Carthaginian takeover of the strait] and viewing it as a necessity not to abandon Messina and thus allow the Carthaginians . . . to build a bridge for crossing over to Italy . . . appointed to the command [of the Messina expedition] one of the consuls, Appius Claudius.

By the time Claudius began marching his army southward toward Rhegium, the Italian city facing Messina across the strait, it was too late. The Carthaginians had already seized Messina's citadel and with it control of the waterway. Saying that the strait fell within the Roman sphere, in 264 Rome accused Carthage of violating the long-standing treaty and declared war. Thus began the terrible death struggle known as the First Punic War.

At first, despite their lack of war fleets, the Romans seemed confident that their land army would ensure them a speedy victory. Claudius commandeered fishing boats and merchant craft and, under cover of darkness, boldly ferried his troops across the strait, managing to slip past the Carthaginian warships. The Carthaginians, who had been confident that their ships would keep the Romans at bay, were taken off guard when they awoke to find Messina surrounded by a Roman army. The Carthaginian commander, Hanno, had no choice but to retreat. Predictably, the Council of Four Hundred had him crucified.

Rome continued its offensive in Sicily, which at first was largely successful. Of particular strategic importance was the decision of the city of Syracuse to ally itself with Rome. But the offensive soon slowed to a halt as Carthage's naval superiority began to take its toll. With the defender's ships blockading Sicilian ports,

This engraving shows Roman warships attacking a Carthaginian fleet.

The Flexible Roman Army

Rome's early republican army was both well organized and efficient. It was divided into units called legions, each with about forty-two to forty-five hundred men. Individual legions varied in structure and featured soldiers of different types, which gave Roman commanders considerable flexibility in planning battle strategies to fit differing situations. The most common overall battle formation, the elements of which often varied in number, type, and position, was called a *quincunx*. In the rear of a basic *quincunx* usually stood about five maniples, or units of 120 men each, comprised of soldiers called *triarii*. These were fighters with extensive battle experience. Spaced in front of the *tri-arii* were perhaps eight, ten, or twelve maniples of *principes*, well-armed troops carrying round shields. In front of the *principes*, stood ten or more maniples of *hastati*, young, vigorous soldiers who carried long, sturdy spears called *hastae*. The strategic logic behind this basic structure of the *quincunx* was first for the *hastati*, who possessed the most stamina, to attack and wear down the opposing soldiers. Then the still fresh *principes* would move forward, replacing the *hastati* and attempting to finish off their tiring enemies. Usually, the *triarii* remained a reserve force who entered the fray only if the *principes* encountered unusual resistance.

A Roman principe *in battle dress.*

A Roman hastatus *in battle dress.*

Rome could not keep its troops adequately supplied, and after four years of inconclusive fighting the Romans made a fateful decision. Realizing that they could not conquer Sicily without war fleets, they endeavored to become a naval power. Here, the Romans clearly illustrated the resourcefulness and adaptability for which they were famous. The shipbuilding project, commented Polybius, "caused them much difficulty, and this fact shows us better than anything else how spirited and daring the Romans are when they are determined to do a thing." In 260 B.C. Roman engineers and carpenters constructed over 120 large naval vessels in a mere two months, an amazing feat considering that they had no prior shipbuilding experience.

The Romans were well aware, however, that just having the ships was not enough. Lacking experienced admirals and crews, they searched for a way to apply their superior land-fighting abilities to sea battles. They found this advantage in a new and clever "secret weapon." R. M. Errington explains:

> One new feature of the Roman ships . . . was the boarding-bridge known as the "raven" (*corvus*). This consisted of a long heavy board mounted upright in the [forward part of the ship], which was fitted with an iron spike on the underside towards the upper end—this was the "beak" of the "raven" which perhaps gave the device its name. At close quarters the board was intended to be dropped on to the enemy's deck, the spike would fasten it into position, and marines could then use it as a bridge for boarding.

Enormous, Chaotic, and Bloody

Eager to test their new naval strength, late in 260 B.C. the Romans, led by the consul Gaius Duilius, attacked a Carthaginian fleet near Mylae, on Sicily's northeastern coast. The Carthaginians saw the unfamiliar superstructures on the enemy decks but had no idea what they were for and entered the battle expecting an easy victory. When they tried to ram the Roman ships, the standard naval tactic at the time, the Romans dropped their deadly ravens. As droves of battle-hardened Roman legionnaires swept onto the Carthaginian ships, the fight became more like a land battle than a sea fight, just as the Romans had hoped. In a stunning defeat, the Carthaginians lost fifty ships sunk and another thirty captured.

Once more confident of certain overall victory, the Romans continued to build ships and to engage the Carthaginians in large-scale sea battles. But as the fighting dragged on for another four years, the Romans once more found that they had underestimated their opponent. Carthage's admirals learned quickly from their mistakes and often managed to avoid contact with the fearsome ravens. During these years, each side lost hundreds of ships and tens of thousands of men in largely indecisive fighting. Finally, in 256, more by sheer tenacity than by skill, Rome managed to gain another clear-cut victory. A Roman fleet of 330 ships and 140,000 men met a Carthaginian force numbering some 350 ships and 150,000 men near Cape Ecnomus in south-central Sicily in what proved to be the greatest naval battle fought in ancient times. The enormous, chaotic, and bloody day-long encounter ended with almost a hundred of Carthage's best ships put out of action and the rest in flight.

(Top) A "crow," or "raven," gangway holds a Roman ship and a Carthaginian vessel together during the huge sea battle of Mylae, fought in 260 B.C. Many thousands of soldiers, crewmen, and oarsmen died in such battles. (Right) The Romans and Carthaginians clash near Cape Ecnomus in southern Sicily in the largest naval battle ever fought in ancient times.

Rome's great victory did more than cripple Carthage's navy. For the first time in the war, the Carthaginians did not have enough ships to guard the North African shore adequately, and the heart of their homeland was wide open to attack. The Romans seized this opportunity and immediately sent to Tunisia an army commanded by the consul Marcus Regulus. The new army landed about seventy-five miles east of Carthage and began ravaging the countryside. The Carthaginians, who had trusted in their fleets and were unprepared for a direct invasion, quickly put their considerable wealth to good use. They hired a skilled Greek general named Xanthippus, who rapidly and expertly trained a combined force of foreign mercenaries and native Carthaginians. In the spring of 255 B.C., Xanthippus led twelve thousand infantry, four thousand cavalry, and about a hundred elephants against Regulus's army of about fifteen thousand infantry and five hundred cavalry. According to Appian's account:

> Regulus, being encamped in the hot season alongside a lake, marched around it to engage the enemy, his soldiers suffering greatly from the weight of their arms, from heat, thirst, and fatigue. . . . Toward evening he came to a river which separated the two armies. This he crossed at once, thinking in this way to terrify Xanthippus, but the latter, anticipating an easy victory over an enemy thus . . . exhausted . . . drew up his forces and made a sudden sally from his camp. The expectations of Xanthippus were not disappointed. Of the . . . men led by Regulus, only a few escaped [and only] with difficulty. . . . All the rest were either killed or taken prisoners, and among the latter was the consul Regulus himself.

From Catastrophe to Victory

Carthage had managed what was at the time a formidable feat. Using mainly mercenaries, it had defeated a contingent of the renowned Roman land army, thwarting what had appeared to be a sure Roman victory in the war. Following this embarrassing defeat, Rome suffered a string of other disasters. In the same year as the defeat of Regulus, the Mediterranean waters ran red with blood as most of the Roman fleet was devastated in a huge storm near the Sicilian coast. Polybius wrote:

> They were overtaken by so fierce a storm and so terrible a disaster that it is difficult adequately to describe it owing to its surpassing magnitude. For of their three hundred and sixty-four ships only eighty were saved; the rest either foundered [capsized] or were dashed by the waves against the rocks and headlands and broken to pieces, covering the shore with corpses and wreckage. History tells of no greater catastrophe at sea taking place at one time.

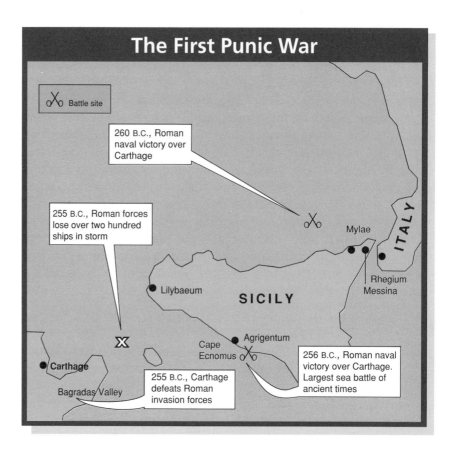

The First Punic War

Battle site

260 B.C., Roman naval victory over Carthage

255 B.C., Roman forces lose over two hundred ships in storm

256 B.C., Roman naval victory over Carthage. Largest sea battle of ancient times

255 B.C., Carthage defeats Roman invasion forces

Mylae

ITALY

Rhegium
Messina

Lilybaeum

SICILY

Cape
Ecnomus

Agrigentum

Carthage

Bagradas Valley

In this and subsequent storms over the next few years, the Romans lost more than seven hundred ships and two hundred thousand men, the worst naval losses ever sustained by any nation in a single conflict.

And yet, Rome, showing its phenomenal ability to endure hardships, stubbornly continued to build fleets and prosecute the war. The Carthaginians proved just as stubborn. About the year 249, the Council of Four Hundred appointed Hamilcar Barca, known as the "man of lightning," to command its forces in Sicily. A brilliant and skilled leader who held a strong hatred for Rome, Hamilcar maintained secret bases in Sicily from which he led lightning raids on the Italian coast. The Romans consistently retaliated, and the fighting dragged on and on, year after year, with neither side able to gain a sustained, decisive advantage.

Finally, after more than two decades of devastating losses of men, ships, and money, the Roman people were exhausted and the nation's treasury empty. There was simply no more public money to build another fleet. But

Hamilcar Barca, Carthage's renowned "man of lightning."

Ancient Warships

For several centuries, the Carthaginian navy was second to none in the Mediterranean. According to ancient historians, Carthage's main warship was the quinquereme, a large vessel which had either five banks of oars or five rowers to an oar. Carthage also used a variety of other designs, including triremes, with three banks of oars, and quadriremes, with four banks.

In a battle, a fully equipped quinquereme probably carried about 300 sailors, of whom 250 to 270 were rowers. The others manned the rigging, masts, and rudders. Such a vessel also carried perhaps 80 to 120 fighting troops, some of them bowmen and catapult operators, who showered enemy ships with missiles; spearmen and swordsmen stood in reserve to defend the ship if the enemy boarded it. The chief offensive tactic in a battle was to use the quinquereme's bow, which was covered by a sturdy bronze "beak," to ram and sink an enemy ship.

Modern scholars are not absolutely certain how such warships were built, but some clues surfaced in 1971. In that year, as historian Peter Connolly explains in his book, *Hannibal and the Enemies of Rome,*

> the hull of a Carthaginian galley was discovered in shallow water just north of the port of Lilybaeum [in Sicily]. This ship, and another which was discovered nearby, have been dated to the period of the first war with Rome. The shipwright's marks on the timbers imply that they were mass produced, which would explain how Rome [whose engineers copied the Carthaginian design] could build 120 ships in two months.

Warships like this one, equipped with both sails and oars, were the mainstay of the Roman and Carthaginian fleets.

A Consul Versus a King

During the Roman campaign against Gaul in 222 B.C., the recently elected consul Marcus Claudius Marcellus became a national hero by defeating the enemy at Clastidium, just south of the Po River. In his *Life of Marcellus*, a part of the larger work *Lives of the Noble Grecians and Romans*, the ancient Greek writer Plutarch recounted how in the midst of the conflict Marcellus met and slew the Gallic leader:

> It was now that the king of the Gauls first saw Marcellus. He guessed from his badges of rank that this was the Roman commander, and . . . he made [headed] directly for him, shouting out a challenge and brandishing his lance. He stood out among the rest of the Gauls, not only for his size, but for his complete suit of armor, which was embossed with gold and silver and decorated with brilliant colors. . . . Marcellus . . . charged the Gaul and pierced his breast-plate with his lance: the impetus [momentum] of his horse hurled his opponent to the ground still living, and a second and a third blow immediately dispatched [killed] him. Thereupon Marcellus leaped from his horse and, laying his hands on the dead man's armor, he gazed up to heaven and cried aloud:

> "Jupiter . . . you who judge the great deeds of generals and captains in war . . . I call upon you to witness that I, a Roman general and a consul, have killed with my own hand a general and a king . . . and that I dedicate to you the first and finest of the spoils. I pray that you will grant us no less good fortune as we fight out the rest of this war."

though the situation seemed hopeless, the proud and resilient Romans refused to accept the idea of defeat. In a grand gesture, unheard of in any other nation, thousands of Romans of all walks of life contributed their own money and valuables to save the state. With this revenue, Roman shipbuilders turned out one last fleet, which confronted the Carthaginians on March 10, 241 B.C., near the Aegates Islands, off Sicily's western coast. The Roman commander, the consul Gaius Catulus, soundly defeated the enemy, sinking fifty Carthaginian ships and capturing seventy more. This proved to be a major disaster for Carthage, which could no longer maintain the fight in Sicily. With the North African coast once again open to attack, the Carthaginians had no choice but to sue for peace.

The victorious Romans exacted harsh terms. According to the treaty ending the war, Carthage had to give up all claims to Sicily, to refrain from sailing its ships into Roman waters, and to pay Rome a huge yearly indemnity, or cash penalty, designed to reimburse the victors for their material losses in the war. These terms crippled Carthage by severely restricting the seafaring empire's ability to maintain its trade network, hence to make money.

Carthage's Troubles

In the years immediately following the war, the Carthaginian merchant rulers found themselves in a desperate situation. As the Picards put it:

> The collapse of the Punic empire was devastating. The Carthaginians . . . [had been] driven out of Sicily; their home territories [had been] laid waste by Regulus and their ports pillaged by privateers [pirates]. Carthage was on the brink of bankruptcy. The royal bank of Egypt was approached for a loan of 2,000 talents, but refused to advance anything, on the grounds of neutrality. . . . The price of peace [war indemnity] was fixed by the Romans at 3,200 talents, or more than fifty tons of silver. The Carthaginian treasury was drained.

Carthage's lack of funds caused it still more trouble and misery. Claiming poverty, the Council refused to pay the agreed amount to the mercenaries it had hired in the war's final years. In retaliation, a formidable force of twenty thousand of these soldiers mutinied and marched on Carthage, initiating a savage, two-year-long struggle known variously as the Mercenary War and the Truceless War. Only through the skill and courage of Hamilcar Barca and a small army of loyal troops was Carthage able in 239 B.C. to defeat the mercenaries and avoid destruction. Its troubles were not over, however, for that same year more of its mercenaries rebelled in Sardinia. When these rebels appealed to Rome for help, the Romans were quick to annex both Sardinia and Corsica, making these valuable islands part of its growing empire. This act amounted to outright theft, but the Carthaginians were helpless; they could neither stop it nor make any other useful response.

For Rome, which in contrast to Carthage enjoyed growth and prosperity in the immediate postwar years, the taking of Sardinia and Corsica was an application of a new national policy. This was a policy of imperialism, the drive to dominate and control other lands, which the recent conquest of Sicily had inspired. Michael Grant points out the effects of this move:

> The annexation of Sicily was a fateful step, for it brought the Romans outside Italy, of which the island was not in ancient times a part, and gave them their first overseas province. An entirely new and lasting stage in Roman history had begun— the epoch [era] of imperialism outside the mother country.

More examples of Roman aggression and expansion followed the Sardinia-Corsica incident. In 229 Rome sent military forces across the Adriatic Sea into Illyria, the rugged, sparsely populated region north of Epirus. The stated goal was to wipe out Illyrian pirates, who had been menacing Adriatic shipping. But Rome's underlying motive was to establish control over Illyria, which it did by building permanent military bases in the region. Soon afterward Rome began a campaign against the Gauls in the Po Valley. This bloody struggle lasted from 225 to 220 and culminated in Roman supremacy in the area, which eventually became a new Roman province known as Cisalpine Gaul. Expansion into Sardinia, Corsica, Illyria, and the Gallic lands both increased Rome's territory and stimulated its economy by enlarging its trade network.

The Barcas in Spain

In the meantime, Carthage, which was slowly recovering from its initial postwar troubles, sought to expand its own economy. Under the command of Hamilcar and his family, who were influential with the ruling Council of Four Hundred, Carthaginian expeditions moved into Spain with the intention of revitalizing the empire's trade and wealth. In retrospect, it is clear that Hamilcar intended to exploit Spain's vast territories, less-advanced native tribes, and rich silver mines to create his own kingdom. While remaining loyal to the mother city, he would build a power base from which to get revenge on the Romans he despised. One day, that is, he planned to attack Rome from the European mainland.

In 237 B.C. Hamilcar began a systematic conquest of Spain and in only a few years controlled most of the lands south of Cape Nao, nearly halfway up the eastern Spanish coast. As he progressed, he enlisted defeated Spaniards into a growing mercenary army. He paid the soldiers well, and they soon comprised the best fighting force in Carthage's long history. During these same years, Hamilcar began to impart his great military knowledge to his brilliant young son, Hannibal Barca. Hamilcar made sure also to instill in the boy a hatred for Rome and all it stood for. According to Polybius, Hannibal later recalled

> that at the time when this father was about to start with his army on his expedition to Spain, he himself, then nine years of age, was standing by the altar, while Hamilcar was sacrificing to [the gods]. . . . Calling Hannibal to him [Hamilcar] asked him kindly if he wished to accompany him on the expedition. On his accepting with delight . . . his father took him by the hand, led him up to the altar, and bade [commanded] him . . . to swear he would never be a friend of the Romans.

It is almost certain that Hamilcar expected his son to one day stand at his side against Rome. But the elder Barca died unexpectedly in 229, leaving his son-in-law, Hasdrubal, in charge of his Spanish kingdom. Hasdrubal continued with the conquest of Spain and established as his main base a town and citadel called New Carthage, about seventy miles south of Cape Nao.

(Left) The young Hannibal, with his father Hamilcar standing behind him, faithfully swears an oath to the Carthaginian gods never to trust or to befriend the Romans. (Below) With his small band of loyal veterans, many of them riding war elephants, Hamilcar Barca brutally destroys the rebellious Carthaginian mercenaries in the Truceless War.

During the years of Hasdrubal's command, Rome became increasingly worried about Carthaginian expansion in Spain. A number of powerful Roman senators voiced their concern that Carthage might extend its dominion northward into Gaul, which would bring it into close proximity with northwestern Italy. Hoping to contain Hasdrubal's expansion, in about the year 226 B.C. the Romans signed an alliance with the independent city-state of Saguntum, located some fifty miles north of Cape Nao.

However, Rome soon found that its alliance with Saguntum was no deterrence to Carthaginian aggression. In 221 Hasdrubal was assassinated by a Spaniard who held a grudge against the Carthaginians, and Hannibal, now in his middle twenties, took command of the Spanish kingdom. Though still relatively young,

Better to Die Fighting

The final stages of Hannibal's siege of Saguntum in 219 B.C. witnessed much misery and loss of life. In this excerpt from his *Roman History*, Appian described how the city's desperate inhabitants displayed both defiance and courage in their last moments:

The Saguntines, when they despaired of help from Rome, and when famine weighed heavily upon them, and Hannibal kept up the blockade without intermission . . . issued an edict to bring all the silver and gold, public and private, to the forum [town square], where they melted it down with lead and brass, so that it should be useless to Hannibal. Then, thinking that it was better to die fighting than starve to death, they made a sally [assault] by night upon the lines of the besiegers while they were still asleep, not expecting an attack, and killed some as they were getting out of bed, and arming themselves with difficulty in the confusion, and others in actual conflict. The battle continued until many of the Carthaginians and all of the Saguntines were slain. When the [Saguntine] women witnessed the slaughter of their husbands from the [city] walls, some of them threw themselves from the housetops, others hanged themselves, and others slew their children and then themselves. Such was the end of Saguntum, once a great and powerful city.

Hannibal Barca (247–183 B.C.) was one of the most brilliant generals of all time. His men saw him as a tower of strength and a hero and gladly risked their lives for him.

Hannibal already enjoyed the respect and devotion of the army, for he was a skilled and inspiring leader with a magnetic personality. The first-century B.C. Roman historian Livy later said of this remarkable individual, "No toil could exhaust his body or overcome his spirit. . . . Both of horsemen and of foot-soldiers he was undoubtedly the first [best]—foremost to enter battle, and the last to leave it when fighting had begun." As to what made Hannibal more able and effective than most other talented commanders, Leonard Cottrell offers this insight in his detailed biography of Hannibal:

The more one scrutinizes his actions the more clear it becomes that every step he took was carefully thought out in advance. Courage and military skill, which he possessed in abundance, would have made him a good company officer or even a divisional commander. But it was his political forethought, his capacity for overall planning and preparation—plus the ability to change his plans quickly when need arose—that made him one of the greatest generals of all time.

Soon after assuming command, Hannibal directed his extraordinary talent for long-range military planning toward a large-scale anti-Roman campaign. Longing to fulfill both his father's and his homeland's desire for revenge against Rome, he decided that the first logical step was to provoke a confrontation. Marching north in 220 B.C., he boldly attacked and besieged Saguntum, which immediately appealed for aid from its new ally, Rome. When Rome demanded a halt to the Carthaginian aggression, Hannibal refused and Saguntum fell to him eight months later. The angry Romans then demanded that the Carthaginian Council surrender Hannibal to Rome. Not surprisingly, the Council, content with the silver and other riches the Barcas had been sending home over the years, rejected the demand. In response, early in 218 Rome declared war. No one at the time, even the far-thinking Hannibal, could have foreseen the immensity, misery, and sheer horror of the conflict that was about to engulf nearly the entire Mediterranean world.

CHAPTER THREE

To the Brink of Ruin and Back: The Second Punic War

For the principal combatants, Rome and Carthage, the Second Punic War proved to be a huge and ruinous battle for survival. It was a seemingly relentless conflict that destroyed almost an entire generation of Roman men in fighting that raged almost to the walls of the two mother cities. The enemy's ability to bring the war directly to the other's native soil came as a rude surprise to both parties. The Romans did not expect Hannibal to attack Italy, for example. He had no fleets in Spain, so he could not sail eastward and land his army on the Italian coast. And the Romans were convinced that the towering, snow-covered Alps constituted a barrier that no army could cross. Since according to this view, Hannibal could not march northward through Gaul and into Italy, his only option was to return to Tunisia and defend his homeland. Yet the wily and audacious Hannibal defied this conventional logic by boldly crossing the Alps in the spring of 218 B.C. As a result of their miscalculation, the Romans would suffer a terrible death toll in the first few years of the war.

Yet Hannibal, too, was guilty of underestimating his enemy. He clearly did not take into account the Romans' tremendous resourcefulness, courage, and adaptability, qualities that allowed them to keep on fighting even after suffering horrendous and crippling losses. Not only would the Romans weather the Carthaginian storm for many years, but, incredibly, they would bounce back and finish by carrying the war to northern Africa. Even with his formidable abilities in strategic planning, Hannibal could not predict that he would one day face the enemy on the Plain of Zama in an encounter that would decide his country's fate as well as his own. Thus, as in the first war between Rome and Carthage, each side's overconfidence led it into unexpected and dangerous circumstances.

Ordeal in the Alps

It is clear from their initial strategy in the war that the Romans did not expect Hannibal to march northward toward the Alps. The Roman plan was to launch a two-part offensive in which one army would attack northern Africa while another marched westward through Gaul and then south into Spain. Hannibal, the Romans reasoned, would eventually be trapped between these two forces. But the Carthaginian leader fully anticipated the Roman strategy and headed it off, leaving Saguntum early in 218 B.C. By April his army of forty to fifty thousand men and thirty-seven elephants had already made it to the Rhone River in southern Gaul, not far from the foothills of the Alps. Hannibal found that his haste had paid off. Just as he was crossing the Rhone, his scouts informed him that Rome's Spain-bound expedition, commanded by the consul Publius Cornelius Scipio, had just landed only fifty miles away, near the river's mouth. Scipio soon learned

Hannibal leads his army across the supposedly impregnable barrier of the Alps mountain range. His exact route is still debated among scholars.

that Hannibal was in the area and hurried north to intercept him. But it was too late. The Carthaginian army had already moved on and begun its fateful Alpine ascent, a maneuver for which the Romans were not prepared.

Hannibal's crossing of the Alps was a feat of daring and endurance that has become legendary. For those who participated, the journey was frightening, dangerous, slow, and miserable. Sometimes giant boulders blocked the narrow passes between mountain peaks and had to be chopped away by hand. Fierce mountain tribes, who did not take kindly to an army of strangers trespassing in their territory, launched periodic ambushes on Hannibal's forces. But worst of all were the numbing cold and the slippery, seemingly endless sheets of snow and ice through which men, horses, and elephants, all carrying heavy loads, had to trudge. Livy recalled the constant

> struggle on the slippery surface, for it afforded them no foothold, while the downward slope made their feet the more quickly slide from under them; so that whether they tried to pull themselves up with their hands, or used their knees, these supports themselves would slip, and down they would come again! . . . The baggage animals, as they went over the snow, would sometimes . . . cut into the lowest crust, and pitching forward and striking out with their hoofs . . . would break clean through it, so that numbers of them were caught fast, as if entrapped, in the hard, deep-frozen snow.

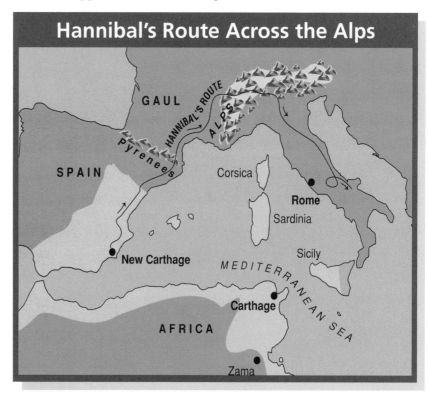

Hannibal's Route Across the Alps

Which Pass Did Hannibal Use?

Modern scholars have tried to reconstruct Hannibal's route through the Alps using as references both works by ancient scholars and recent geological studies. For instance, a coordination of ancient and modern data helps to reveal whether the main pass Hannibal used was high or relatively low in altitude. According to Polybius's account, the ancient Alpine passes were snow-filled all year long. Today, the average snow line in the Alps lies between nine thousand and ten thousand feet. The climate has changed since the time of the Second Punic War, however: Geological records indicate that the ancient snow line was lower—six to seven thousand feet. This explains how a route that is largely snow-free today would have been choked with snow and ice over two thousand years ago and thus might have been the one used by Hannibal.

Of the major passes that lie roughly between southern France and northwestern Italy, most scholars believe the Montgenèvre, now in eastern France near the Italian border, is likeliest to be the one Hannibal chose. As historian Peter Connolly argues, the Montgenèvre fits most of the descriptions given by Polybius, Livy, and other ancient scholars. It has a level area at the summit large enough for an army to camp on. The pass also has a steep descent, matching ancient records that go into considerable detail about the troubles the Carthaginians encountered on their way down. Also fitting the ancient descriptions, the Montgenèvre pass's far side lies about three day's march from the leading edge of relatively flat land.

Having led his troops to the southeastern slopes of the Italian Alps, Hannibal points toward their goal—the lush countryside of the Roman-controlled Po Valley.

The Novelty of War Elephants

Hannibal brought some three dozen war elephants with him over the Alps. All but one of these died in the crossing or during the first winter in northern Italy, and the Carthaginian general thereafter rode the lone survivor in his initial victory parades. Carthage's use of war elephants was not unique in the Mediterranean world. The army of Alexander the Great encountered these beasts when it invaded India in the fourth century B.C. In the following century, many Middle Eastern and Mediterranean realms, including Egypt, Epirus, and Carthage, began importing elephants from India for use in battle. In time, Carthage found it increasingly expensive to import Indian elephants and started hunting a slightly smaller native variety, the North African forest elephant, a species now extinct.

In battle, elephants were most often ef-fective against troops and horses that had never seen them before. For example, the formidable bulk, strange odors, and frightening trumpeting sounds of Pyrrhus's elephants caused panic in the Roman ranks during the Battle of Heraclea in 280 B.C. The beast also proved effective in Carthage's victory over Regulus's army during the Roman invasion of northern Africa in 255 B.C. Here, the elephants both frightened and trampled many Roman legionnaires. Elephants were also useful as pack animals because they could carry or drag large loads of military supplies. In time, the Romans and other peoples who did not utilize elephants grew accustomed to them and also learned how to kill them with well-placed spear thrusts. The animals thereby lost their novelty and effectiveness and few nations used them after 100 B.C.

An engraving shows a war elephant in combat. Though these beasts proved initially effective by creating panic among troops who had never encountered them before, they eventually lost their novelty and ceased to be used in battle.

After the terrible, fifteen-day-long ordeal in the Alps, Hannibal entered the Po Valley and assessed his losses. His forces now numbered only about twenty thousand foot soldiers, six thousand cavalry, and a few elephants. Yet he remained confident. First, he had accomplished his goal of surprising the Romans. They were now scrambling to respond to his sudden appearance in northern Italy. Scipio, who had sent his army on to Spain to prevent any more Carthaginian armies from marching into Gaul, was now in command of a Roman force organizing to move on Hannibal. The other consul, Tiberius Sempronius Longus, had been in Sicily preparing to invade Tunisia when he learned of Hannibal's bold maneuver. Longus now rushed his men northward, hoping to reinforce Scipio before Hannibal marched south. Hannibal also felt confident because he expected rebellion from many of the subject peoples recently conquered by Rome. The Gauls, Samnites, and others, Hannibal reasoned, would see him as a liberator and join his ranks. He was sure that without the manpower of these defeated peoples to support it, Rome's Italian power base would collapse.

Rome's Troubles Begin

The Romans hoped to strike a quick and decisive blow against Hannibal before the Carthaginian general could incite rebellions or do any other damage. To that end, in late December 218 B.C. Scipio and Longus joined up on the south bank of the Po, creating a combined force of some forty-four thousand men that gave them clear numerical superiority over the enemy. But sheer numbers were not enough to defeat their crafty foe. Early one morning, Hannibal sent a cavalry detachment to the Roman camp near the Trebia River, a southern tributary of the Po. Instead of attacking, the horsemen pretended to lose their nerve and then to retreat, which drew the Romans out of their camp and into Hannibal's deadly trap. According to Appian, the Romans crossed the river that separated the hostile armies

> on a raw sleety morning . . . wading in the water up to their breasts. . . . When the battle was joined, the horses of the Romans, terrified by the sight and smell of the elephants, broke and fled. The foot-soldiers, although suffering much and weakened by cold, wet clothes and want of sleep, nevertheless boldly attacked these beasts . . . and were already pushing back the enemy's infantry. Hannibal, observing this, gave the signal to his horsemen [who had been waiting in ambush] to outflank the enemy.

Beset by attacks from both front and rear, the confused Romans broke ranks and retreated to the river, where the Carthaginians slaughtered many of them.

Owls, Bees, and Flaming Meteors

Most ancient peoples were strongly superstitious and believed in omens, supernatural signs foretelling that something important, either good or bad, was going to happen soon. The Romans were no exception. In this excerpt from *Punica*, his epic poem about the Second Punic War, the Roman writer Silius Italicus lists some of the evil omens that supposedly preceded Rome's terrible defeat at Cannae in 216 B.C. Although a few of the signs related may have been exaggerated versions of real events, many are clearly fanciful and were probably invented by later Romans attempting to shift the blame for the infamous defeat to the gods and fate.

When the Romans reached Cannae, built on the site of a former city, they planted their doomed standards [national emblems] on a rampart of evil omen. Nor, when such destruction was hanging over their unhappy heads, did the gods fail to reveal the coming disaster. Javelins blazed up suddenly in the hands of astounded soldiers . . . [and] many a screech-owl beset the gates of the [Roman] camp. Thick swarms of bees constantly twined themselves about the terrified standards [bearers], and the bright hair [tail] of more than one comet, the portent [omen] that dethrones monarchs, showed its baleful glare. Wild beasts also in the silence of night burst . . . into the camp, snatched up a sentry before the eyes of his frightened comrades, and scattered his limbs over the adjacent fields. Sleep also was mocked by terrible images: men dreamt that the ghosts of the Gauls were breaking forth from their graves. . . . A dark stream of blood flowed in the temples of Jupiter. . . . In the southern sky, bright meteors shot against Italy from the direction of Africa; and the heavens burst open with a fearful crash, and the countenance [image] of the Thunderer [Jupiter] was revealed.

The defeat at the Trebia marked only the beginning of Rome's troubles. Impressed with Hannibal's victory, many local Gauls joined him, increasing his numbers to as many as fifty thousand. He then marched south to Lake Trasimene, just seventy miles north of Rome, and in the spring of 217 met another Roman army, this one commanded by a new consul, Gaius Flaminius Nepos. As at the Trebia, Hannibal used a clever ambush to surprise his opponents. The noises raised in this large and desperately fought battle near the lake were said to be so loud that none of the soldiers were aware of a great natural disaster happening at the same time. "At the very crisis of the battle," wrote the ancient Greek/Roman historian Plutarch, "an earthquake occurred, in which cities were overthrown, rivers diverted from their channels, and fragments of cliffs torn away. And yet . . . not one of the combatants noticed it at all." In a decisive defeat, the Romans lost fifteen thousand men killed and another fifteen thousand captured. By contrast, Hannibal's casualties were minimal.

Hannibal's Gigantic Death Trap

Demoralized, the Romans fully expected the victorious Hannibal to march on Rome next. In desperation, they activated a rarely used emergency provision that allowed the government to appoint a "dictator," a single individual with total authority over the country. A dictator was expected to save the state from impending disaster in six months, and then step down. In this crisis, the Romans chose Fabius Maximus, an aristocrat known for his honesty and sound judgment. Fabius immediately destroyed the bridges leading to Rome and prepared the city for a siege.

But the siege never came, as once more Hannibal did what his enemy least expected. He wisely reasoned that besieging such a large city would take too long, draining his army's strength. The Romans could keep themselves well supplied via the Tiber River, but Hannibal had no ships and no effective siege equipment—for reasons that remain unclear, the Carthaginian Council of Four Hundred did not see fit to send Hannibal such vital hardware at the height of his success in Italy. Most important, Hannibal realized that taking and keeping Rome would require a strong supply base in the countryside. But this was impossible without widespread rebellion of Rome's subject peoples, which had still not occurred. So Hannibal headed away from Rome and into south-central Italy.

The Romans now wondered what to do about this formidable enemy in their midst. Although most Romans seemed to favor the idea of pursuing and punishing the Carthaginians, Fabius decided against this tactic. Feeling that Rome had lost too many men to Hannibal, he chose instead the more cautious policy of following the enemy around the countryside, harassing and skirmishing with the Carthaginians but never engaging them in full-scale battle. The goal was to wear down Hannibal while denying him the satisfaction of a victory.

But though the guerrilla strategy seemed to work, public opposition to such measures steadily increased, and citizens demanded that Fabius attack and exact revenge on Hannibal. After Fabius's term as dictator ran out in 216 B.C., two new consuls—Gaius Terentius Varro and Lucius Aemilius Paullus—were elected, and they reversed Fabius's policy. With an army of sixty to seventy thousand men, the consuls marched to Cannae, in southwestern Italy, where Hannibal was camped with about forty to forty-five thousand troops. By this time, Hannibal's army was composed of what the Romans saw as a bizarre mixture of nationalities, including soldiers from Carthage, Numidia, Spain, Gaul, and the Po Valley. On August 2, 216, the two armies clashed, and once more Hannibal displayed his tactical genius. Military historian Peter Connolly describes the Carthaginian general's strategy and the battle:

When Hannibal saw the Roman forces drawn [lined] up he sent out his pikemen [soldiers carrying long spears] and light-armed troops as a covering force, and behind these he drew up the rest of his army. . . . He advanced his center to form a crescent to break the force of the Roman charge. On the right wing he placed his Numidian horsemen and on the left his Celtic [Gallic] and Spanish cavalry. . . . As usual the battle was begun by the light-armed [troops] and the cavalry. On the left wing the Carthaginian horsemen tore into their opponents. . . . Relentlessly, the Romans were driven back. . . . Then both sides charged. The Romans crashed into the center of the crescent. On and on they thrust until they had flattened the formation and still they came on. . . . Hannibal had accomplished his master plan. The [Romans] pushed his center back so far that they passed the African pikemen on either wing. . . . The pikemen now faced inwards and charged the Roman flanks. The Celtic and Spanish cavalry left the Numidians to complete the destruction of the [Roman] cavalry and attacked the legions in the rear.

Hannibal's Carthaginians and mercenaries surround and annihilate the Romans at Cannae, in what proved to be the most devastating defeat that Rome ever experienced.

Unable to escape from Hannibal's gigantic death trap, the Romans, though most fought gallantly, were overwhelmed and annihilated. In this, the single worst military defeat in its long history, Rome lost over fifty thousand men, including the consul Paullus and about eighty senators. Hannibal lost six thousand men, far fewer by comparison.

Lucius Aemilius Paullus, who served as one of Rome's consuls in 219 B.C. and again in 216, meets his death on the bloody field of Cannae.

The Romans Slowly Recover

After his mighty victory at Cannae, it seemed to many people inside and outside Italy that Hannibal was invincible and that Rome was doomed. Some Italians, including many Samnites and the residents of the prosperous city of Capua, located about a hundred miles southeast of Rome, finally rebelled and joined Hannibal. Syracuse in Sicily also allied itself with Hannibal, threatening Roman control of the island Rome had fought so hard to wrest from Carthage in the First Punic War. Although most of Rome's other subject peoples remained loyal, the Romans also found themselves at war with another foreign power. This was Macedonia, the powerful kingdom that encompassed most of Greece. Its king, Philip V, assuming that Hannibal would defeat Rome, allied himself to Carthage in 215 B.C. Philip then planned to invade eastern Italy and began massing men and supplies in Illyria.

But even with all these new allies, Hannibal could not deal Rome to a quick defeat. For one thing, he still had no ships, no siege equipment, and no reinforcements from his homeland. The Carthaginian Council had apparently concluded that it was wiser to send men and supplies to Spain, where the Carthaginians and Romans battled on a second front. So besieging the city of Rome remained too impractical and risky a venture for Hannibal. Also, after Cannae the Romans decided that Fabius had been right all along and they resumed the former dictator's famous delaying tactics. Frustrated, Hannibal had to roam around Italy, foraging for food and burning towns when he could, while unable to goad the Romans into handing him any more decisive victories.

Meanwhile, the resilient Romans began to recover from their losses. As they had in the climax of the first war, all Roman classes joined ranks and supported the state with both loyalty and money. They continued to raise and train new armies for the attempt to wear Hannibal down, and slowly began reconquering the subjects who had rebelled. In 212 B.C., for instance, the Romans captured Syracuse. And the following year they retook Capua, beheaded its leaders, and enslaved the inhabitants as a warning to other would-be deserters. At the same time, Roman forces kept the Macedonians at bay in Illyria and prevented them from invading Italy.

Rome's resurgence was also evident in Spain. There, Publius Scipio and his able brother Gnaeus fought their way down the coast and in 211 captured Saguntum, the city whose fall had started the war. Both Scipios died in battle soon afterward, Gnaeus losing his life while fighting an army under Hasdrubal Barca, Hannibal's brother. According to Livy:

> As for Gnaeus Scipio, some relate that he was slain on the hill in the first onset [attack] of the enemy, others that with a few men he made his escape to a tower near the [Roman] camp; the fire was lighted around this, and so, by burning the doors which they had been unable to force in any way, [the Carthaginians] captured the tower and all were slain in it along with the commander himself.

Despite these losses, the Romans gave up little ground, for the new commander of Rome's Spanish campaign, Publius Scipio's son of the same name, was a brilliant and skillful general. He captured New Carthage in 209. And a year later, leading his army against Hasdrubal's forces at Baecula in central Spain, he forced the Carthaginians into retreat.

The War's Turning Point

In a way, Hasdrubal's retreat in Spain set in motion a chain of events that eventually led to the clash at Zama and the end of the war. Instead of remaining in Spain and waiting for the younger

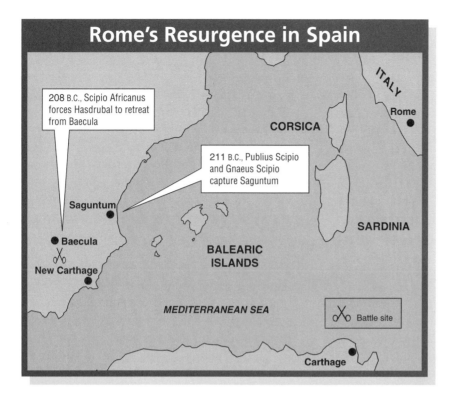

Rome's Resurgence in Spain

208 B.C., Scipio Africanus forces Hasdrubal to retreat from Baecula

211 B.C., Publius Scipio and Gnaeus Scipio capture Saguntum

CORSICA

ITALY

Rome

Saguntum

Baecula

New Carthage

BALEARIC ISLANDS

SARDINIA

MEDITERRANEAN SEA

Battle site

Carthage

Scipio to finish him off, Hasdrubal marched his army northward, eluded a Roman force guarding the route into Gaul, and made for the Alps. His goal was to bring his brother the reinforcements he had been denied so long. Together, Hasdrubal reasoned, the Barcas would defeat Rome once and for all. Hasdrubal sped across Gaul and, crossing the Alps by an easier route than his brother had used, and in milder weather, descended into the Po Valley in 207 B.C. The appearance in Italy of a new Carthaginian army numbering some thirty thousand men sent a wave of fear and apprehension through the Roman ranks, which nevertheless rose once again to the challenge. Leonard Cottrell explains:

> As soon as they knew that Hasdrubal was moving towards Italy the Romans prepared to meet the shock of two Carthaginian armies in their territory. Hannibal was in the south. Hasdrubal would obviously approach from the north. . . . If the two greatest sons of Hamilcar Barca managed to combine their armies in the heart of Italy, then the outlook for the Romans would be black indeed. To meet this double threat, the republic made the most gigantic effort in twelve years of bitter fighting.

The Roman consul Gaius Claudius Nero, who had been shadowing Hannibal in the south, led seven thousand hand-picked men on a forced march northward. He soon joined a larger force, made up of every fighting man Rome could muster at that crucial moment, commanded by Marcus Livius. This combined

Rome's Sword and Shield

In addition to his exploits in the Gallic wars during the 220s B.C., Marcus Claudius Marcellus held the office of consul five times, successfully besieged and retook Syracuse after the Sicilian city joined Hannibal, and also distinguished himself as a leader in Italy during the years that Hannibal roamed the countryside at will. In this famous tract from his *Life of Marcellus*, Plutarch compares Marcellus to another leader who was later remembered as a national hero—Fabius Maximus:

> After Hannibal had invaded Italy, Marcellus was sent to Sicily in charge of a fleet. Then came the disastrous defeat at Cannae, in which thousands of Romans were killed. . . . At this point Marcellus dispatched fifteen hundred men from his fleet to help defend Rome. . . . By this time the Romans had lost the greater number of their generals and prominent men in battle, while Fabius Maximus, who had earned the highest reputation for his reliability and shrewdness of judgment, was blamed for his excessive caution. . . . The people regarded him as a general who was perfectly qualified to carry on a defensive campaign, but who could never move over to the offensive. They therefore turned to Marcellus, and in the hope of combining his boldness and energy with Fabius's caution and foresight, they sometimes elected both as consuls together and sometimes sent out one as consul and the other as pro-consul [former consul sent to do a specific job]. . . . Fabius was called the shield and Marcellus the sword of Rome. And indeed Hannibal himself declared that he feared Fabius as a schoolmaster and Marcellus as an opponent. The first prevented him from inflicting losses on the Romans: the second inflicted them on him.

army surprised Hasdrubal near the Metaurus River in northeastern Italy and in a desperate and hard-fought battle decisively defeated the Carthaginians. Hasdrubal died fighting, and the Romans chose a particularly gruesome way to deliver this news to his brother. A few days later, they tossed Hasdrubal's severed head into Hannibal's camp.

Although Hannibal remained in Italy for four more years, it became increasingly clear that Carthage's cause was lost. The Romans, having journeyed to the brink of ruin and back, seemed to rebound on all fronts. They captured all of Spain by 206 and the following year eliminated the Macedonian threat by signing a treaty with King Philip. Late in 205, Scipio, now a national hero thanks to his exploits in Spain, established a huge base of operations in Sicily in preparation for an invasion of Tunisia. With his homeland in jeopardy, Hannibal could not continue to devote himself to small-scale operations in Italy, and finally he made the decision to abandon that land. As he knew full well, his departure marked a great, and for him sad, turning point in the war. Comments R. M. Errington:

> The safety of Italy was now assured. Whether Scipio won or lost the final battle . . . it was inconceivable that [the outcome] would persuade the Carthaginian Council that any advantage could be gained form Hannibal's returning to Italy. The war was not yet over; but its most dangerous sector (for Rome) had been firmly closed.

CHAPTER FOUR

A Battle of Giants: Hannibal and Scipio at Zama

Scipio Africanus made his name fighting in Spain before coming to blows with the formidable Hannibal.

On the Plain of Zama, not far from Carthage, the great death struggle between Rome and Carthage finally reached its climax. Here, after nearly sixteen years of desperate fighting, what were at the time the world's two greatest powers met to decide the fate of Mediterranean civilization. On the eve of battle, the Carthaginians suffered from a number of clear disadvantages. First, the enemy had invaded their homeland and now threatened their mother city. In the long war, Carthage had lost Spain and other important supply bases, which the Romans now exploited. In addition, the Carthaginians had lost nearly all their allies, including the Macedonians, the Syracusans, and the Gauls, and now stood alone against a revitalized and expanded Rome. For Carthage, then, the battle represented a last-ditch effort to save itself from overall defeat.

The one advantage Carthage possessed, the wild card it hoped would produce the miracle it needed, was Hannibal, already a legend in his own time. The remarkable general, now in his middle forties, had never been defeated. Once recalled from Italy, the Carthaginians reasoned, he might turn the Roman invasion into a retreat, as Xanthippus had done in the first war. Yet no one knew better than Hannibal that this new threat to his homeland was far more dangerous than the earlier one. This time the Romans were commanded by Scipio, a leader comparable in talent and skill to

Alexander, Pyrrhus, and Hannibal himself. As the opposing forces moved toward their inevitable confrontation, it became increasingly obvious that the coming fight would be less a test of national strengths and more a clash between two individuals. In this battle of giants, the great Hannibal would finally meet his match.

Scipio Invades Africa

Scipio had no political rival among his own countrymen. Riding high on the wave of popularity generated by his Spanish triumphs, he was the darling of most senators and common citizens alike. After easily winning the election as consul in 205 B.C., he urged and won governmental approval of a direct invasion of Tunisia. The following spring, his forces, numbering about thirty thousand, departed Sicily and landed near Utica, a walled port city about twenty-five miles northwest of Carthage. Scipio immediately began a siege of Utica, planning to use its harbor as a landing point for supplies and reinforcements.

Scipio also enlisted the aid of a local Roman ally, a Numidian leader named Masinissa, who had been periodically fighting the Carthaginians for some time. Masinissa was a tough, intelligent commander whose crack unit of Numidian horsemen was famed throughout the Mediterranean. Together, in 204 and on into 203, Scipio and Masinissa easily defeated a number of small, badly trained Carthaginian and Numidian forces that tried to stand up to them.

Eventually, Scipio increased the pressure on Carthage by ravaging the countryside around the capital. Realizing that a siege was imminent, the Council of Four Hundred decided to recall Hannibal. In the meantime, in an apparent attempt to stall for time while Hannibal crossed into Africa, the Council offered Scipio a truce, supposedly to begin peace negotiations. Scipio accepted and while the negotiations proceeded, Hannibal landed his army at Leptis, some one hundred miles southeast of Carthage.

For Hannibal, leaving Italy had been emotionally difficult. "They say," wrote Livy, "that rarely has any other man leaving his country to go into exile departed so sorrowfully as Hannibal on withdrawing from the enemy's land." Leonard Cottrell offers this explanation:

> When he had entered Italy he was twenty-nine. Now he was forty-five. . . . From youth to middle age Italy had been his home, and it is said that his sorrow at leaving his beloved Apulia [the fertile southern Italian region in which he camped for years] was great. He had kept the oath which he had sworn at his father's side—to remain an enemy of Rome—but that enemy was still undefeated, and after his brother's death on the Metaurus [River], he told his fellow officers that he "foresaw the doom of Carthage." So it must have been with a heavy heart that he landed again in his homeland.

A bust depicts Hannibal. He raised a force of more than forty thousand men in the spring of 202 B.C. to repel the Roman invasion force led by Scipio.

Surrender or Fight

In Hannibal's first few months in Africa, he focused his attention on gathering his forces for the coming struggle. His veterans from the Italian campaign now numbered only a few more than twenty thousand, not nearly enough to stand up against the Romans. He therefore sent messengers to ask former allies for help. Tychaeus, a Numidian chief friendly with Carthage, sent two thousand horsemen, and the Carthaginian general Mago arrived with twelve thousand troops he had raised in Liguria, a region of southern Gaul. Philip of Macedonia, once again betting that Hannibal would win, sent about four thousand men, a violation of his treaty with Rome he would later regret. Counting scattered local Carthaginians who flocked to his side, by the spring of 202 B.C. Hannibal had a mixed force of mercenaries and Carthaginians totaling perhaps forty to forty-five thousand men. He also had eighty elephants, more than he had used in any previous battle. Estimates for Scipio's strength at the time, including Masinissa's cavalry, range from thirty-six to forty thousand.

Hannibal made the first move by leaving his base of operations at Hadrumetum, on Tunisia's eastern coast, and marching his army westward in pursuit of Scipio. This suited Scipio well, for he had been planning to lure Hannibal away from his supply base anyway. A few days later, Hannibal's scouts reported that the Romans were camped at the town of Zama, located on the edge of a plain of the same name about seventy-five miles southwest of Carthage. After making camp a safe distance from the enemy, the Carthaginian leader sent out some scouts to spy on the Romans, who promptly captured three of these agents. To Hannibal's surprise, a few hours later the scouts rode unhurt into the Carthaginian camp. Scipio had given them a grand tour of the Roman camp and released them, which in effect constituted a message to Hannibal that the Roman leader was so confident of victory that he did not mind revealing his troop strength.

Hannibal was so impressed by Scipio's audacity that he requested a meeting with his Roman adversary. Scipio eagerly accepted, and the next day a small escort of horsemen from each camp crossed a deserted section of the plain to converge at the designated site. Hannibal and Scipio then walked forward, accompanied only by interpreters, and gazed upon each other for the first time. "For a moment they remained silent," Livy recalled, "looking at each other and almost dumbfounded by mutual admiration."

Then the two men conversed, although their exact words are unknown. According to Polybius's later reconstruction, based on the testimony of the interpreters, Hannibal declared, "Would that neither the Romans had ever coveted any possessions outside Italy, nor the Carthaginians any outside Africa." He supposedly went on to ask Scipio if there was any way they could resolve their differences without fighting. Scipio then reportedly insisted that the fault for this war, as well as the last, lay with Carthage, not Rome. In invading Italy and slaughtering thousands of Romans, Scipio pointed out, Hannibal had not stopped to consider a peaceful solution. Why should the Romans do so, now that the tables were turned? "What remains to be done?" asked Scipio. "Put yourself in my place and tell me." Hannibal stood silent, acknowledging that Scipio's point was a valid one. "Of what further use then is our interview?" Scipio asked. "Either put yourselves and your country at our mercy or fight and conquer us." With that, the two greatest generals in the world parted and returned to their armies, their differences to be resolved in blood.

Forming Ranks

At daybreak on the following morning, the opposing generals assembled their forces into huge formations facing each other across the plain. Scipio placed Masinissa and his Numidian horsemen on his right wing. On the left wing stood a contingent of Italian cavalry commanded by Gaius Laelius, a Roman admiral and Scipio's close friend, who was as at home on a horse as at the helm of a ship. Between these cavalry units stretched the armored infantry, the bulk of the Roman army. Scipio deployed his three rows of maniples in an unusual way. Instead of forming alternating squares like a checkerboard, as was most common, the maniples of each row stood directly behind those in front, creating open lanes running from the army's front to its rear.

The clever Scipio had two reasons for arranging his troops in this fashion. First, he hoped that most of Hannibal's elephants would run down the cleared lanes instead of trampling Roman troops. Second, the lanes would allow Scipio's light-armed troops, the *velites*, or skirmishers, to run back and forth through the lines at will. The skirmishers, who usually numbered about twenty to each maniple and wore little or no armor, carried several spears. Their job was to run up to the enemy line, hurl their weapons, and then fall back behind the cover of the heavily armored infantry. Polybius reported details of the plan:

> The intervals of [lanes between] the first maniples [Scipio] filled up with cohorts of *velites*, ordering them to open the action, and if they were forced back by the charge of the elephants to retire, those who had time to do so by the straight passages as far as the rear of the whole army, and those who were overtaken to [fall back to the] right or left along the intervals between the lines.

Hannibal formed his ranks differently. In the front, he placed his elephants, which he hoped would scare the Roman horses and also break up some of the maniple ranks. Behind the elephants the infantry stood in three long parallel lines, separated by perhaps two hundred feet. In the front line were the Gauls and Ligurians, along with assorted foreign skirmishers. The second line consisted of better trained and more experienced fighters, most of them Carthaginians and other Africans. In the rear line stood Hannibal's Italian veterans, his best troops, and on the wings, to the far left and right of the infantry, were cavalry contingents that faced their Roman counterparts.

A Deafening Noise

After Hannibal and Scipio delivered their final battle speeches, which were designed to lessen fear and raise enthusiasm in their respective forces, an eerie silence descended on the field. For a long moment, only occasional grunts from the animals broke the calm, as the men in the opposing armies eyed each other apprehensively. Then the silence was shattered by the blasts of war trumpets sounding the charge. "Hannibal first ordered the trumpets to sound," wrote Appian, "and Scipio responded in like manner. The elephants began the fight decked out in fearful panoply [brightly colored body coverings] and urged on . . . by their riders."

No sooner had the elephants' charge begun, however, when it faltered. Following Scipio's prior order, the Roman trumpeters continued blasting away and the troops raised their voices in loud battle cries. This deafening noise terrified many of the elephants, which turned around and collided with the front Carthaginian lines. Some of the horses in Hannibal's right wing stampeded. Seeing this, Laelius immediately charged his horsemen into the confused opposing cavalry.

Meanwhile, some of Hannibal's elephants kept up their forward motion and crashed into the *velites* in the forefront of the Roman maniples. A few of the beasts even trampled some of the infantrymen who stood behind the skirmishers. But the damage was relatively light, for most of the frightened elephants sought

The formation of the Roman ranks at Zama. Note the cavalry units massed on the wings and the rectangularly shaped maniples arrayed, one behind the other, between them.

The Amazing Numidian Horsemen

In the Battle of Zama, as well as in other battles, both the Carthaginians and the Romans utilized Numidian cavalry. Numidia, the region of northern Africa now called Algeria, was renowned for its warrior horsemen. In battle, the Numidians skillfully maneuvered their steeds, often darting in and around enemy infantry formations and hurling spears at the foot soldiers. They also charged into opposing cavalry units, where they engaged in hand-to-hand fighting with enemy riders or attempted to knock them off their horses. The Numidians' most effective tactic was to chase down fleeing soldiers and thrust with spears at the desperate runners. Groups of Numidians accomplished this task with devastating efficiency under Hannibal at Cannae and later under Scipio at Zama.

In addition to being formidable fighters, the Numidian horsemen could cover great distances quickly with little food and water, eluding pursuers by hiding in ravines and caves. Their prowess as riders was all the more amazing when one considers that they had neither saddles nor bridles, both of which make it easier for a rider to stay on and to control the horse. These ancient riders used only a simple neck strap, which they held with one hand while they threw their spears with the other. On the arm holding the strap a Numidian carried a small round shield, but to keep his horse's load as light as possible, he wore no other armor.

the quickest escape routes, which were the lanes between maniples, created by Scipio for just that purpose. As the beasts lumbered along, skirmishers showered them with spears. Some of the wounded elephants collapsed in agony, but a few went berserk, reversed direction, and charged into the Carthaginian left wing. Masinissa took advantage of the chaos this created by attacking the enemy horsemen with his mounted troops. Both Carthaginian wings now spun around and at top speed galloped across the battlefield, with Masinissa and Laelius in hot pursuit.

While the receding cavalry units raised a huge cloud of dust, and soon disappeared behind it, the two massive opposing infantry formations now converged on each other. According to Polybius:

> Both formations slowly and in imposing array [orderly ranks] advanced on each other, except the troops which Hannibal had brought back from Italy, who remained in their original position. When the formations were close to each other, the Romans fell upon their foes, raising their war-cry and clashing their shields with their spears as is their practice, while there was a strange confusion of shouts raised by the Carthaginian mercenaries [who spoke many different languages].

Scipio's Foresight

As the infantry stage of the battle began, the battle-hardened Roman legionnaires easily cut their way through the less-experienced Gauls and Ligurians in Hannibal's front line. Hannibal had ordered the men in the second Carthaginian line to hold firm in their ranks no matter what. So this solid wall of armored men refused to open up, even to allow the retreating Gauls to run through. As a result, many Gauls were crushed or impaled between the converging Roman and Carthaginian lines; the few who managed to crawl to safety fled the field.

The fight between the Romans and the troops of the second Carthaginian line was long and hard fought. During the savage exchange, men from Scipio's rear maniples moved around their fighting comrades and then on around the sides of the Carthaginians. Once they had outflanked and trapped their opponents, the Romans methodically slaughtered most of them. The surviving Carthaginians retreated to Hannibal's third line, his huge formation of veterans who constituted the cream of his army. These formidable troops refused to break ranks, and many of the retreating second-line Carthaginians, like their Gallic comrades in an earlier stage of the battle, had to escape by running sideways between the opposing battle lines.

At this juncture, Scipio saw that his front line was shorter than that of Hannibal's line of veterans. The Roman commander

immediately understood that the Carthaginians might now out-flank and envelop their opponents, as the Romans had just done. In a brilliant spontaneous maneuver, Scipio ordered his trumpeters to sound the recall, and his highly disciplined troops fell back at once. Quickly, Scipio rearranged his men so that they formed a long, gapless line equal in length to the enemy's.

Seconds later, the Romans and Hannibal's veterans converged again. "Thus began an entirely new battle," said Livy. "For [the Romans] had reached the real enemy, their equals in character of their weapons and their experience in war and the celebrity of their deeds." Here, the Romans were at a slight disadvantage, for by this time most of them were tired, while their opponents were fresh. If this final infantry engagement had gone on without interruption, Hannibal's veterans would have had an even chance of overcoming the Romans.

But owing to Scipio's foresight, the complexion of the battle suddenly changed once again. In his original plan, which was inspired by Hannibal's strategy at Cannae, Scipio had called for Masinissa and Laelius to destroy the enemy cavalry and then swing around and outflank the Carthaginians. Thus it was that after pursuing the Carthaginian horsemen for miles and defeating them, Masinissa and Laelius returned to execute another pivotal part of Scipio's plan. Leonard Cottrell takes up the story:

The Carthaginian elephants charge the Roman lines in the first stage of the Zama battle. The Romans showered spears onto the beasts' huge torsos, killing many and driving others into a panicked stampede.

Before long, the sound of hoofs and the war cries of the Numidian and Roman horsemen were heard above the tumult [commotion], as the returning commanders took the Carthaginians in the flank and rear. Then it was Cannae in reverse. The battle became a massacre, and though most of Hannibal's veterans fought grimly on, they were cut to pieces.

Indeed, the slaughter was so terrible that according to Polybius, the attacking Romans were hindered by "the quantity of slippery corpses which were still soaked in blood and had fallen in heaps and the number of arms thrown away haphazard."

The Plans of Valiant Men

When the devastating struggle finally ended, Scipio and his commanders inspected the battlefield and assessed their victory. At least twenty thousand Carthaginians had been slain and another twenty thousand or so were now Roman captives. By contrast, Roman troop losses, including Masinissa's Numidians, were probably not more than four thousand killed, although a much larger number undoubtedly were wounded.

Hannibal himself managed to escape with a handful of followers and rode full speed to his base at Hadrumetum. He was sure that at least for the moment, Scipio would not pursue him there. The Roman commander would have his hands full seeing to the needs of his victorious army, providing for the prisoners of war, and negotiating with the Council of Four Hundred to secure the

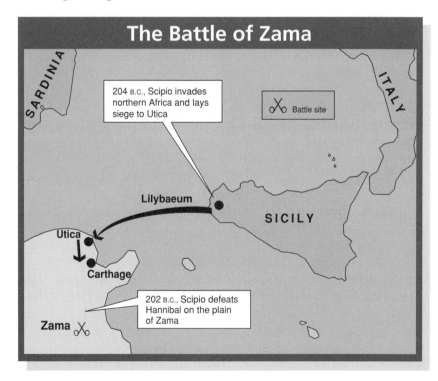

The Battle of Zama

204 B.C., Scipio invades northern Africa and lays siege to Utica

Battle site

SARDINIA

ITALY

Lilybaeum

SICILY

Utica

Carthage

202 B.C., Scipio defeats Hannibal on the plain of Zama

Zama

Surpassing Alexander

Modern scholars who study the evolution of warfare have noted that by the time of the Battle of Zama, the Romans, influenced by the Greek armies in the eastern Mediterranean, had adopted many aspects of the Macedonian fighting system. But they had also made their own improvements, as military historian Archer Jones explains in his book *The Art of War in the Western World*.

> The Macedonian system as used by Alexander [the Great, in the fourth-century B.C.] became the standard for the eastern Mediterranean and much of the old Persian empire [in what is now the Middle East]. The difference between the Macedonian and Roman systems lay not primarily in the Roman use of swords and the Macedonian reliance on the spear; the difference was . . . [that] the Macedonian system. . . relied on the combined effect of all arms, including a cavalry force trained for real shock combat. . . . The role of the cavalry in the Roman victory at Zama revealed that the Romans had adopted the Macedonian system. But the use of a reserve [force] by both combatants and the superior articulation [troop arrangement] that made this possible shows that the art of war had surpassed that of Alexander's era. Neither Hannibal nor Scipio had participated in the battle, both remaining where they could manage the contest and commit their reserves at the critical time and place. This represented a major advance over Alexander's preplanned battles [in which he himself fought in the ranks and therefore could not significantly alter the plan once the battle was engaged]. . . . The excellent articulation of the Roman army had done much to permit Scipio to command all of the army in battle rather than, as had Alexander, only a part.

surrender of Carthage. After all, by destroying the ability of Carthage to resist, Scipio's triumph at Zama had ended the war in Rome's favor. Scipio had no real desire to kill or capture Hannibal. For the younger general, the glory and prestige of having given the great Hannibal his first taste of defeat would be satisfying enough. Whether Hannibal was ashamed or depressed about his defeat, remains unknown. But even his enemies later expressed the opinion that he had nothing to be ashamed of. Polybius summed up the general view, saying:

> He had done in the battle and before it all that could be done by a good general of long experience. For, in the first place, he had by his conference with Scipio attempted to terminate the dispute by himself alone . . . and was fully aware of the part that the unexpected plays in war. In the next place, when he offered battle he so managed matters that it was impossible for any commander with the same arms at his disposal to make better plans for a contest against the Romans than Hannibal

did on that occasion. . . . Hannibal had shown incomparable skill in adopting at the critical moment all such measures as were in his power and could reasonably be expected to succeed. . . . If he, who had never as yet suffered defeat, after taking every possible step to insure victory, yet failed to do so, we must pardon him. For there are times when Fortune counteracts the plans of valiant men, and again at times, as the proverb says, "A brave man meets another braver yet," as we may say happened in the case of Hannibal.

Pupil Becomes Teacher

While in reality Scipio was no braver than Hannibal, he had shown himself to be a brilliant general who knew well how to exploit his own forces for maximum effect. Scipio had also demonstrated how great commanders advance the art of war by adopting and building on the innovations of their predecessors. At Cannae, Hannibal had perfected the maneuver of enveloping an army's wings and surrounding the entire body, and at Zama Scipio used a variation of the same tactic to defeat its originator. The pupil had become the teacher.

Unsurprisingly, after Zama Scipio did not chase after his opponent, but rather, occupied himself with the duties of a triumphant Roman commander. According to Appian:

> Now, Scipio, having gained this splendid victory, prepared himself for sacrifice, and burned with his own hands, as is the custom of the Roman generals, the less valuable spoils of the enemy. He sent to Rome ten talents of gold, 2,500 talents of silver, a quantity of carved ivory, and the most distinguished of the captives in ships, and Laelius to carry the news of the victory. The remainder of the spoils he sold, and divided the proceeds among the [Roman] troops.

When Laelius reached Rome with the news, the citizens joyously celebrated the war's end. But they reserved the full depth and intensity of their adulation for Scipio himself. Zama's outcome made him a national hero of epic proportions, and when he returned to Rome he entered the city in the most stupendous triumph, or victory parade, Rome had ever witnessed. Preceded by trumpeters, elephants, incense bearers, musicians, and a number of shackled Carthaginian prisoners, Scipio, Appian wrote, appeared, "on a chariot embellished with various designs, wearing a crown of gold and precious stones, and dressed, according to the fashion of the country, in a purple toga interwoven with golden stars. He bore a scepter [staff] of ivory, and a laurel branch, which is always the Roman symbol of victory." In recognition of his successful African campaign, the Romans gave Scipio the name "Africanus," by which he was known thereafter.

Gold, Crowns, and Laurel Branches

One of the most colorful and impressive events in ancient Rome was the victory triumph, a huge parade to celebrate winning a battle or war. Scipio's triumph after his victory at Zama was more spectacular than any that preceded it, as recalled by Appian in his *Roman History*.

The form of the triumph (which the Romans still continue to employ) was as follows: All who were in the procession wore crowns. Trumpeters led the advance and wagons laden with spoils. Towers were borne along representing the captured cities, and pictures [huge drawings] showing the exploits of the war; then gold and silver coin and bullion, and whatever else they had captured of that kind; then came the crowns that had been given to the general as a reward for his bravery by cities, by allies, or by the army itself. White oxen came next and after them elephants and the captive Carthaginian and Numidian chiefs. Lictors [officers bearing Roman insignia] clad in purple tunics preceded the general; also a chorus of harpists and pipers, in imitation of the Etruscan procession, wearing belts and golden crowns, and they march in regular order, keeping step with song and dance. . . . Next came a number of incense-bearers, and after them the general himself on a chariot. . . . Then followed those who had served him in the war as secretaries, aides, and armor-bearers. After these came the army arranged in squadrons and cohorts, all of them crowned and carrying laurel branches, the bravest of them bearing their military prizes. . . . When Scipio arrived at the Capitol [hilltop dominated by a great temple to Jupiter] the procession came to an end, and he entertained his friends at a banquet in the temple, according to custom.

Scipio (standing in chariot), newly dubbed "Africanus," rides with his troops in his magnificent victory triumph.

In their moment of elation and relief at winning the long, devastating war, few Romans considered the possibility that the Carthaginians would ever trouble them again. But in fact, though defeated, the city-state of Carthage still possessed abundant human and material resources. And the mighty city itself, along with its magnificent harbors, had escaped a destructive siege and was still very much intact. That meant that Carthage would inevitably recover from its defeat and regain its power. In a few short decades, the Romans would once more come to perceive Carthaginian power as a threat. And this time they would put an end to that threat in a manner unprecedented in its coldness and brutality.

CHAPTER FIVE

The Eagle Triumphant: Carthage's Gallant Last Stand

The main events of Roman-Carthaginian relations following the Battle of Zama tell the sad story of the demise of a great nation and the lonely death of its most distinguished citizen. The Romans had feared Hannibal when he had ravaged Italy at the height of his power. After his defeat, that fear turned to distrust and suspicion, for Rome still saw Hannibal as a potential danger. The renowned general was still in his prime and might conceivably conspire with Rome's enemies, forcing a new generation of Roman soldiers to give their lives to stop him.

Likewise, the city of Carthage remained splendid and undamaged, despite its decisive defeat and the harsh peace terms exacted by Rome. According to the treaty imposed by Scipio, the Carthaginians had to give up all claims to Spain and their Mediterranean island possessions. They had to recognize Rome's ally Masinissa as king of Numidia and allow the Romans to burn all but ten of their warships. In addition, Carthage was forced to pay a yearly war indemnity of two hundred talents for a period of fifty years and to pledge not to wage war against anyone without Rome's permission.

Yet the Romans knew full well that the Carthaginians could build more ships. They could revive some of their old trade routes, create new ones, and make alliances with nations outside of Rome's influence. Thus, Carthage clearly possessed the potential, just as it had at the end of the first war, of rising from its defeat and once more challenging Roman supremacy. The highly practical Romans were not about to risk reliving the devastation they had suffered from Hannibal and from Carthage. And so, because they posed a potential threat to Rome, man and city alike were doomed.

Roman Expansion Continues

Rome's worries and suspicions about Carthage after the conclusion of the Second Punic War were to some degree understandable. With its great victory, Rome had become the undisputed master of the western Mediterranean. It now controlled Italy, Sicily, Sardinia, Corsica, Illyria, Spain, and southern Gaul, and its influence also extended over most of northern Africa. Having become the strongest nation on earth, Rome could not afford to allow a third-rate power, which Carthage now was, to threaten its new empire.

That empire was destined to continue expanding, for the more territory Rome seized, the more imperialistic it seemed to become. Almost immediately after beating Carthage, the Romans turned their attention eastward toward Greece and the Middle East. Their first target was Macedonia's King Philip, who now had to pay the price for helping Hannibal at Zama. In 200 B.C., under the leadership of Scipio Africanus and the consul Titus Flaminius, Rome launched a campaign against Macedonia that pitted the Roman and Greek military systems against each other. The three-year

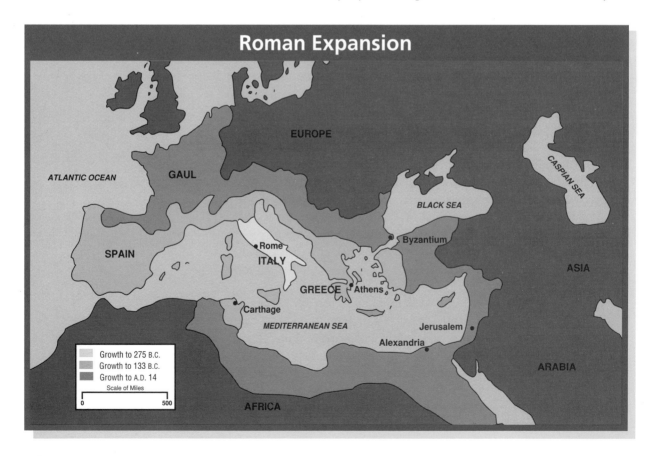

Roman Expansion

Growth to 275 B.C.
Growth to 133 B.C.
Growth to A.D. 14

conflict ended with a major Roman victory at Cynoscephalae, in northern Greece, in May 197. During the battle, according to Michael Grant,

> Philip's right wing charged successfully downhill but was then engaged in the rear by the Romans and routed [defeated], and the Macedonian cause was lost. In this first direct conflict between two different military traditions, the new flexibility taught by Scipio Africanus [and used by him at Zama] had made the legions more than a match for the tightly packed and relatively immobile Greek phalanx. In its defeat, the future of the eastern Mediterranean world could be read without too much difficulty.

Indeed, the other Greek-ruled kingdoms in the east soon met the same fate as Macedonia. In 193, Antiochus III, ruler of the Seleucid kingdom, which then encompassed Syria, Palestine, and other sections of the Middle East, defied the Romans by seizing a portion of northern Greece. The Romans responded promptly. They drove Antiochus from Greece and in 190, at Magnesium in Asia Minor, they delivered him a disastrous defeat. Other Roman conquests followed, and the last Greek-ruled kingdom, the Ptolemaic, consisting principally of Egypt, came under Rome's dominion in 167. All these eastern realms became Roman vassal states, which meant that they could manage their own local affairs as long as they supported and obeyed Rome.

The Architect of Victory

Though heavily involved in its eastern campaigns, Rome still kept a close eye on both Carthage and Hannibal. In the few years directly following Zama, Carthage was hard put to pay the yearly war indemnity and concentrated all its energies on reviving its crippled economy. The defeated empire did not seem to pose an immediate threat to Rome. In the meantime, Hannibal worked diligently with members of the Council of Four Hundred to help rebuild the wealth and influence of Carthage. It is doubtful that during these years the general planned to raise more armies and threaten Rome. In fact, he displayed what seemed like a sincere desire to maintain the peace dictated by his former enemy.

Yet the talented and resourceful Hannibal proved so successful at reviving Carthaginian prosperity that the Romans once more felt threatened by him. That threat seemed all the more real when, in 195 B.C., a group of Hannibal's political opponents in Carthage secretly sent word to the Roman Senate that he was plotting with Antiochus of Seleucia to attack Rome, a charge that was almost certainly false. When Roman officials arrived in Carthage, supposedly to confer with the Council, Hannibal guessed that they had come for him and prepared his escape. In his work, *The Book of the Great Generals of Foreign Nations,* the Roman historian Cornelius Nepos recorded that diplomatic representatives

> came to Carthage from Rome. Hannibal thought that they had been sent to demand his surrender; therefore, before they were given audience by the Council, he secretly embarked on a ship and took refuge with King Antiochus in Syria. When this became known, the Carthaginians [in order to stay in Rome's good graces] sent two ships to arrest Hannibal, if they could overtake him; then they confiscated his property, demolished his house from its foundations, and declared him an outlaw.

By running directly to Antiochus, with whom he had been accused of plotting, Hannibal only made himself look more guilty to the Romans. Perhaps Hannibal realized that Rome was out to destroy him at any cost and that appearances no longer mattered. In any case, the Seleucid king was one of the few Mediterranean rulers willing to risk Rome's wrath by harboring the famous fugitive.

It was at Antiochus's court in Ephesus that Hannibal once more met his old nemesis Scipio. In 193, on the eve of war with Seleucia, the eminent Roman, at the moment playing the role of ambassador, had come to learn what he could about Antiochus's war aims. Perhaps at a banquet, Scipio and Hannibal conversed at length. Not surprisingly, the topic of conversation eventually turned to military leaders and strategy, and according to Livy,

> when Africanus asked who, in Hannibal's opinion, was the greatest general [of all times], Hannibal named Alexander [the Great], the king of the Macedonians, because with a small force he had routed armies innumerable. . . . To the next request, as to whom he would rank second, Hannibal selected Pyrrhus, saying that . . . no one had chosen his ground or placed his troops more discriminately [using better judgment]. . . . When [Scipio] continued, asking whom Hannibal considered third, he named himself without hesitation. Then Scipio broke into a laugh and said, "What would you say if you had defeated me?" "Then, beyond doubt," Hannibal replied, "I should place myself both before Alexander and before Pyrrhus and before all other generals."

Not long after paying Scipio this supreme compliment, Hannibal had to leave Antiochus's court, for Roman agents still pursued him. They chased him from country to country for ten more years until they finally cornered him in 183 in a house in Bithynia, in northern Asia Minor. Seeing that there was no escape, Hannibal, now sixty-five and tired of running, drank poison. Livy

Downfall of the Scipios

After having been one of Rome's most renowned and prestigious families for over thirty years, the Scipios experienced a serious reversal of fortunes beginning in 188 B.C. After that year, the annually elected consuls were not friends and supporters of Scipio Africanus, as they had been for many years; rather, they came mainly from the ranks of his political opponents. These new consuls, as well as a number of senators, felt that Scipio was too soft in his proposals for the treatment of foreign and Italian subject peoples. So they attempted to lessen the great general's influence over the government by discrediting him. Led by Marcus Porcius Cato, known as Cato the Elder, or the Censor, Scipio's enemies continually accused him and some of his relatives of various illegal acts. In 187, for example, the government appointed a special investigator to look into charges against Scipio's brother Lucius, who had helped Rome to win the Battle of Magnesium against the Seleucids in 190. According to Cato and others, Lucius had embezzled a large sum of public money. Africanus himself was accused of negotiating the treaty with Carthage in 201 to his own advantage.

It is highly unlikely that any of these cases had any merit, and apparently none came to trial. However, Cato and his cronies managed to tarnish the Scipio name and reputation beyond repair, and the family's influence waned. The angry Scipio Africanus went into seclusion and shortly before he died in 182 ordered the following inscription for his tombstone: "My ungrateful country shall not have my bones." After the death of Cato three decades later, the Scipios regained some of their popularity with the ascendancy of Scipio Aemilianus, Africanus's adopted grandson and the destroyer of Carthage.

Scipio and his brother Lucius stand before the senators to face various charges, including embezzling public funds. No trial or conviction followed the charges, but the negative publicity badly damaged the family name.

Finding himself trapped by Roman agents bent on his destruction, the mighty Hannibal takes his own life by swallowing poison.

reported his last words as, "Let us now put an end to the great anxiety of the Romans, who have thought it too lengthy, and too heavy a task, to wait for the death of a hated old man." Thus, the architect of the great victories at Cannae and Lake Trasimene, a man who had once held in his hands the fate of Europe, died a pauper and an outlaw in a little-known foreign land. Scipio died the following year at the age of fifty-three.

A Remarkable Degree of Restraint

Roman hatred and distrust of Carthaginians did not die with Hannibal. In Roman eyes, Carthage, which had regained much of its former prosperity, remained a potential threat to the stability of the region. For a long time Rome did little or nothing about this threat, mainly because Carthage steadfastly honored the terms of the peace treaty. It paid its war debt regularly, built no more warships, and refrained from making war on anyone.

That the Carthaginians managed to abide by their pledge not to fight showed that they possessed a remarkable degree of restraint, considering that they were frequently under attack. Beginning about 200 B.C., Masinissa, who believed that his alliance with Rome would protect him, made periodic raids of Carthaginian fields and villages. Rather than retaliate, after each raid Carthage followed protocol and appealed to Rome to arbitrate the matter. But the Romans, still wanting to punish their old enemy any way they could, invariably sided with the Numidian. After each incident, wrote Appian, "the Romans sent envoys to restore peace, telling them as before to help Masinissa secretly. They artfully confirmed Masinissa in the possession of what he had already taken, in this way."

In 154 Masinissa, now in his eighties but still vital, committed his boldest aggression yet by capturing a fertile farming area about seventy-five miles from Carthage. Carthage made its customary appeal to Rome, and the following year a delegation was sent. The chief Roman negotiator was Marcus Porcius Cato, an influential senator who in his youth had fought as a soldier against Hannibal. In his eighties, his hatred of the Carthaginians intact, Cato was, according to Plutarch,

> a man who observed the ancestral custom of working his own land, who was content with a cold breakfast, a frugal dinner, the simplest clothing, and a humble cottage to live in, and who actually thought it more admirable to renounce luxuries than to acquire them.

For the conservative and miserly Cato, widespread prosperity and consumption of material goods, such as he witnessed on his trip to Carthage, seemed outrageous and immoral, especially in a city that had been responsible for so many Roman deaths. In his biography of the Roman senator, Plutarch wrote:

> It was at once apparent to Cato that the city was by no means crushed nor impoverished. . . . He found it teeming with a new generation of fighting men, overflowing with wealth, amply stocked with weapons and military supplies of every kind, and full of confidence at this revival of its strength. He drew the conclusion that this was no time for the Romans to occupy themselves with regulating the affairs of Masinissa and the Numidians, but that unless [the Romans] found means to crush a city which had always borne them an undying hatred . . . they would find themselves as gravely threatened as before.

Rome's New War

Upon his return to Rome, Cato began to convince his fellow senators, many of whom were staunch conservatives like himself, that Carthage once more represented a dire threat. He aggressively called for military action, ending every speech, no matter what the subject, with the phrase *Delenda est Carthago!* ("Carthage must be destroyed!"). In time, most Roman leaders

Cato and the Figs

After visiting Carthage in 153 B.C., Cato the Elder returned to Rome in a huff. He had for decades harbored a hatred for Rome's former enemy, and seeing Carthaginian prosperity firsthand had only reinforced that animosity. Convinced that Rome should attack and eradicate Carthage, Cato set out to win the support of his colleagues in the government. According to Plutarch in his *Life of Cato*, the elderly senator chose a dramatic way to begin his anti-Carthaginian crusade: he delivered a lengthy speech outlining what he had seen in Carthage, how the Carthaginians possessed many weapons of war, and how they once more posed a threat to Roman security.

As he ended this speech, it is said that Cato shook out the folds of his toga and contrived to drop some Libyan [North African] figs on the floor of the Senate-house, and when the senators admired their size and beauty he remarked that the country which produced them [Carthage] was only three days' sail from Rome. Afterwards he adopted a still more forceful method of driving home his point: whenever his opinion was called for on any subject, he invariably concluded with the words, "And furthermore it is my opinion that Carthage must be destroyed!" . . . This is the way in which Cato is said to have brought about the third and last war against Carthage. He died almost immediately after it had begun.

Marcius Porcius Cato, called "the Elder," the conservative Roman politician who convinced his colleagues to destroy Carthage once and for all.

came to agree with Cato, and they made a secret decision to attack and demolish Carthage. The plan was to wait for a legal excuse, some Carthaginian violation of the treaty that still existed between the two nations, to ensure that Carthage could be blamed for the outbreak of yet another war.

Masinissa soon provided the excuse the Romans were looking for. In 151 B.C. he laid siege to the Carthaginian town of Oroscopa and a few months later, in 150, the Carthaginian general Hasdrubal (unrelated to previous leaders of that name) retaliated. On a plain somewhere in western Tunisia, Hasdrubal's forces engaged those of the Numidian king in a large pitched battle. The outcome was indecisive, but Masinissa later surrounded his opponent's camp, starved the Carthaginians into submission, and massacred most of them as they surrendered. Even though Masinissa clearly had been the aggressor, Roman leaders seized on this opportunity. Charging that by fighting the Numidians, Hasdrubal had "made war without Roman permission," thereby violating the treaty, in March 149 the Romans declared war.

About two months later, a Roman army crossed from Sicily to Utica, which had recently and prudently abandoned the cause of Carthage and offered the use of its harbor to Rome. Leading this invasion force of about eighty thousand infantry and four thousand cavalry were the consuls Manius Manilius and Marcius Censorinus. Apparently, the Romans were not content to launch an immediate attack on the Carthaginians, who repeatedly insisted that they had no desire to fight. Choosing first to use psychological warfare, the Romans issued a series of cruel and humiliating demands. Deceitfully, however, they allowed the Carthaginian envoys to believe that if these demands were met, the city might be spared. The first demand was that Carthage hand over to the consuls three hundred children from the city's leading families. After deciding that they had no choice, the Carthaginians complied. Appian told how

> they sent their children [into Roman hands] amid the tears of the parents, the kindred, and especially the mothers, who clung to their little ones with frantic cries and seized hold of the ships and of the officers who were taking them away, even holding the anchors and tearing the ropes. . . . Some of them even swam out far into the sea beside the ships, shedding tears and gazing at their children. Others on the shore tore out their hair and pounded their breasts as though they were mourning the dead.

Indeed, in the eyes of their loved ones the children were as good as dead. Manilius and Censorinus ordered the hostages to be shipped to Rome, and their ultimate fate remains unknown.

The consuls soon made a second demand, ordering Carthage to surrender all of its armor, weapons, and catapults. Again, the Carthaginians complied. And then came the final, most humiliating demand. The consuls insisted that the inhabitants of Carthage abandon immediately their city by the sea and begin building new homes at least ten miles inland. The Romans would then proceed to raze, or demolish, the entire city.

Carthage's End

Upon hearing this outrageous third demand, the citizens of Carthage decided that they had had enough of Roman bully tactics. A new mood of defiance suddenly gripped the city as people from all walks of life banded together and heroically rose to the challenge. According to Appian's account, "A wonderful change and determination came over them to endure everything rather than abandon their city. Quickly all minds were filled with courage from this transformation." The Carthaginians turned temples and other buildings into emergency workshops in which they worked day and night turning out swords, shields, catapults, and other weapons. Meanwhile, Hasdrubal, who commanded a force outside the city, prepared to meet the Roman menace. The Romans did not expect such a formidable show of force and at first suffered a number of embarrassing defeats. For over a year, the Carthaginians continually repulsed the consuls' attempts to besiege the city and even managed to defeat a large Roman force in open battle.

But this desperate display of courage was ultimately of no avail. Early in 147 B.C. the Romans placed Scipio Aemilianus, adopted grandson of Scipio Africanus, in charge of the war effort in Africa. After resupplying and regrouping Roman forces, the able Scipio began a long and bloody siege of Carthage. Though the defenders fought gallantly, Roman might, efficiency, and relentlessness proved too much for them. In March 146 Scipio's legionnaires entered the city, and six days of savage street fighting followed. Stubbornly defending to the death every house and building, the Carthaginians—men, women, and children alike—suffered terrible atrocities and died by the tens of thousands. Finally, obeying the orders of the Roman Senate, Scipio ordered the whole city put to the torch. At one point during the seventeen days in which the fire burned, Scipio stood on a nearby hilltop and stared out at the huge inferno. His friend, the historian Polybius, who stood beside him, recorded the moment:

> At the sight of the city utterly perishing amid the flames, Scipio . . . burst into tears and stood long reflecting on the inevitable change which awaits cities, nations, and dynasties, one and all, as it does every man. This, he thought, had befallen . . . the once mighty empires of the Assyrians, Medes, Persians [all in western Asia], and that of Macedonia, lately so splendid. . . . And turning to a friend who stood near him, he

grasped his hand and said: "It is a wonderful sight, but, I know not how, I feel a terror and dread lest someone should one day do the same to my own native city."

When the deadly fire burned itself out, the Romans razed the city and sold the few remaining survivors into slavery. To discourage anyone from ever again building there, they plowed salt into the whole site and its surrounding fields and placed a curse on the area. Thus, wrote Appian, "this city, which had flourished 700 years . . . and had ruled over so many lands, islands, and seas, as rich . . . as the mightiest empires . . . now came to its end in total destruction." Thereafter, what had been the city-state of Carthage became the Roman province of Africa.

Roman soldiers cock a catapult during the final siege of Carthage. The Romans, masters of the art of siege warfare, also employed spear-shooting devices, tall scaling ladders, battering rams, and wooden siege towers against the Carthaginian battlements.

Carthage's Last Fleet

One of the most ingenious and daring feats in the annals of warfare took place during the final siege of Carthage in 147–146 B.C. The Roman commander, Scipio Aemilianus, ordered his men to build a mole, or earthen dike, across the outer entrance to the city's harbors. This would seal off the city and also afford the legionnaires a platform on which to mount battering rams to breach the defensive walls. While the mole was under construction, the Carthaginians hatched a bold plan. According to Appian, they secretly "began to excavate another entrance on the other side of the harbor facing the open sea. . . . Even the women and children helped to dig. They began the work inside and carefully concealed what they were doing." Simultaneously, behind the high wall that surrounded their naval base, they constructed about fifty warships, using whatever wood they could scrounge from within the city. Finally, Appian reported, "everything being finished, the Carthaginians opened the new [harbor] entrance about dawn, and passed out with fifty triremes. . . . The Romans were so astounded by the sudden appearance of . . . the fleet . . . that if the Carthaginians had at once fallen upon their ships, they might have possessed themselves of the whole [Roman] fleet." But the Carthaginians chose only to sail around in a defiant show of force and then return to the city. Three days later they sallied forth again and this time attacked the Romans. But it was too late, for Scipio had taken advantage of the time to prepare his own ships. Carthage's last fleet suffered defeat, and soon Scipio finished his mole, sealing the city's fate.

The Path to the Future

Carthage's demise marked the end of three devastating Punic Wars, conflicts caused mainly by greed—that of Carthage for wealth and that of Rome for power and territory. The Mediterranean could not accommodate two such soaring ambitions and so one was doomed to extinction. Though it struggled mightily, and under the brilliant Hannibal nearly prevailed, in the end Carthage, like so many other proud lands before and after it, fell before the triumphant Roman eagle.

Indeed, after destroying Carthage in 146 B.C., Rome continued its policy of conquest and expansion. In that same year, the Romans also razed the Greek city of Corinth and imposed direct rule on the former Greek kingdoms. And in the following century the Roman general Julius Caesar invaded and conquered most of Gaul and even made landings in southern Britain. Then, in the wake of ruinous civil wars, in the 30s B.C. the Roman Republic fell. That did not mark the end of Roman power, however, for under a succession of emperors the political system that came to be called the

Roman Empire lasted for another five hundred years and dominated most of the world known to Europeans.

But Rome's dominion could not last forever. The empire slowly crumbled and, fulfilling Scipio's prophecy of doom, in A.D. 476 fell under the onslaught of less culturally advanced peoples from central and northern Europe. Many small, loosely organized kingdoms dotted the former Roman Empire in the following centuries, and some of them eventually grew into modern nations such as Britain, France, and Germany. These nations retained Rome's considerable cultural legacy, including its architecture and its legal and political ideas; the Latin language, as well, was used by educated people long after the development of modern English, French, and so on.

Thanks to Rome's thorough annihilation of its longtime enemy, Carthage left behind no such cultural legacy. Sad to state, Carthage's great public buildings, magnificent harbors, and splendid villas, along with nearly all of its arts, crafts, literature, and native histories, vanished forever. Luckily, Greek and Roman writers such as Polybius, Appian, Livy, and Nepos recorded the stirring tale of Carthage's rise and fall. Otherwise, the glory of Carthaginian civilization, including Hannibal's remarkable military deeds, would remain virtually unknown to the present day.

The pitiful ruins of Carthage, once one of the world's greatest cities, continue to bake and crumble under the hot Tunisian sun.

Marveling at Hannibal's deeds, it is tempting to wonder what might have happened if Carthage had won rather than lost the Second Punic War. A Carthaginian victory would certainly have been likely if, after Cannae, Hannibal had possessed the siege equipment he needed to take Rome. And victory over Scipio at Zama might have allowed Carthage to rebound, eventually producing a similar outcome. If so, European civilization would surely have developed very differently, with markedly different concepts of law and justice, and perhaps with modern languages based on Phoenician instead of Latin. From such speculation emerges an important lesson. The actions of both governments and powerful individuals, be they successes or failures, have consequences that affect countless generations to come. In this way the triumphs and tragedies of the past help to carve out the path to the future.

For Further Reading

Lionel Casson, *Daily Life in Ancient Rome*. New York: American Heritage, 1975. A fascinating presentation of how the Romans lived: their homes, streets, entertainments, eating habits, theaters, religion, slaves, marriage customs, government, tombstone inscriptions, and much more.

Peter Connolly, *Hannibal and the Enemies of Rome*. Morristown, NJ: Silver Burdett, 1978. A comprehensive, easy-to-read study of the history and military customs of the Carthaginians, Gauls, and other traditional Roman opponents. Contains many fine illustrations of costumes, weapons, and battles.

Leonard Cottrell, *Hannibal: Enemy of Rome*. New York: Holt, Rinehart and Winston, 1961. Cottrell, a well-known archaeologist and scholar, provides an excellent, well-researched account of Hannibal and the Second Punic War, including much insight by ancient scholars and the author himself on the great Carthaginian's character. Somewhat advanced reading.

Harold Lamb, *Hannibal: One Man Against Rome*. New York, Bantam, 1963. A highly comprehensive and very readable telling of the Punic Wars, with a main emphasis on the second conflict and Hannibal's exploits. Somewhat advanced reading.

Anthony Marks and Graham Tingay, *The Romans*. London: Usborne, 1990. A beautifully illustrated summary of Roman history and all aspects of daily life, written for basic readers.

Claude Moatti, *The Search for Ancient Rome*. New York: Abrams, 1993. A fascinating and beautifully illustrated overview of how modern researchers unearthed various aspects of Roman civilization. Includes impressive reconstructions of what the Forum and other sections of Rome looked like in their heyday.

Don Nardo, *The Punic Wars*. San Diego: Lucent Books, 1995. In a book that can be used as a companion volume to this one, the author provides a comprehensive overview of the Punic Wars, including more detail on military campaigns in Spain, Sicily, Illyria, and elsewhere, as well as numerous primary source descriptions by Greek and Roman authors.

———, *The Roman Republic* and *The Roman Empire*. San Diego: Lucent Books, 1994. Comprehensive, easy-to-read overviews of Roman civilization, covering its entire span, from the city's founding in 753 B.C. to the empire's fall in A.D. 476.

Chester G. Starr, *The Ancient Romans*. New York: Oxford University Press, 1971. A general survey of Roman history with several interesting sidebars on such subjects as the Etruscans, Roman law, and the Roman army. Also contains many primary source quotes by ancient Greek and Roman writers.

Works Consulted

Appian, *Roman History*. Translated by Horace White. Cambridge, MA: Harvard University Press, 1964. The eleven surviving books of this second-century A.D. Roman historian's twenty-four-volume telling of Roman history, thoughtfully researched and clearly written, remain essential reading for any serious student of Roman times.

Donald Armstrong, *The Reluctant Warriors*. New York: Crowell, 1966. A detailed, well-written summary of the Punic Wars by a noted military historian.

James Henry Breasted, *Ancient Times: A History of the Early World*. Boston: Ginn, 1944. Although somewhat dated, this remains one of the best general sources on ancient civilizations. Extremely well researched, well organized, and entertaining.

Gavin de Beer, *Hannibal: Challenging Rome's Supremacy*. New York: Viking Press, 1969. A detailed, somewhat scholarly study of the Second Punic War that is fairly easy to read. Contains several helpful maps, a feature missing from many similar histories.

R. M. Errington, *The Dawn of Empire: Rome's Rise to World Power*. London: Hamish Hamilton, 1971. A detailed and very insightful study of Roman imperialism from 264 to 146 B.C., the period of the Punic Wars and Roman expansion into Gaul, Spain, Illyria, northern Africa, and Greece.

Lucius Florus, *Epitome of Roman History*. Translated by Edward S. Forster. Cambridge, MA: Harvard University Press, 1960. Florus, of whom little is known, derived much of his material from Livy's history of Rome but undoubtedly used other sources now lost. Although the *Epitome* is told with an obvious pro-Roman bias, it is still one of the more important ancient sources on Rome.

Michael Grant, *History of Rome*. New York: Charles Scribner's Sons, 1978. As with Grant's many other studies of Greek and Roman times, this volume is very comprehensive, insightful, and well written. The section on the Punic Wars is certainly as fine an overview of that topic as can be found anywhere.

Silius Italicus, *Punica*. Translated by J. D. Duff. Cambridge, MA: Harvard University Press, 1961. This work by the first-century A.D. Roman poet is the longest surviving Latin poem, containing about twelve thousand verses. The subject is the epic Second Punic War, including its heroes—Hannibal, Fabius Maximus, and Scipio Africanus. This is difficult reading, recommended strictly for scholars.

Archer Jones, *The Art of War in the Western World*. New York: Oxford University Press, 1987. A scholarly study of the weapons and techniques of warfare in history. Contains excellent detailed descriptions of Roman soldiers and legions, as well as tactics and outcomes of several important battles, including Zama.

Livy, *History from the Founding of the City*. Translated by Frank Gardner Moore. Cambridge, MA: Harvard University Press, 1966. Of Livy's magnificent 142-volume study of Roman history, from the founding to about 9 B.C., only thirty-five volumes survive. But these are among the most important ancient sources for the Punic Wars and many of Rome's other conflicts. Extremely worthwhile reading for those interested in Roman history.

Dorothy Mills, *The Book of the Ancient Romans*. New York: G. P. Putnam's Sons, 1927. This well-researched summary of ancient Roman culture, supported by many long primary source quotations, is old but not particularly dated.

Cornelius Nepos, *The Book of the Great Generals of Foreign Nations*. Translated by John C. Rolfe. Cambridge, MA: Harvard University Press, 1960. This important ancient source by the first-century B.C. historian is similar thematically to, but smaller than, Plutarch's *Lives* and contains biographical sketches of Hamilcar Barca and Hannibal, among others.

Gilbert Picard and Colette Picard, *Daily Life in Carthage at the Time of Hannibal*. New York: Macmillan, 1961. A very detailed and scholarly study of Carthaginian customs, ideas, and cities.

————, *The Life and Death of Carthage*. New York: Taplinger, 1968. The companion book to the Picards' *Daily Life*, this equally scholarly study covers the political and social events of Carthage's history.

Plutarch, *Life of Marcellus, Life of Fabius Maximus*, and *Life of Cato the Elder,* taken from *Lives of the Nobel Grecians and Romans* in *The Makers of Rome*. Translated by Ian Scott-Kilvert. New York: Dorset Press, 1985. Excellent translations of Plutarch's biographies. For those interested in other aspects of Roman history, this volume includes Plutarch's lives of Coriolanus, Tiberius, and Gaius Gracchus, Sertorius, Brutus, and Marc Antony.

————, *Life of Pyrrhus* and *Life of Fabius Maximus*, in *Lives of the Noble Grecians and Romans*. Translated by Bernadotte Perrin. Cambridge, MA: Harvard University Press, 1958. Plutarch's biographies of important classical figures were based on many ancient sources that are now lost. Although the author sometimes showed pro-Greek and pro-Roman biases, his works are thought to be reasonably accurate.

Polybius, *The Histories*. Translated by W. R. Paton. Cambridge, MA: Harvard University Press, 1966. A long and very detailed telling of Roman history during the period of the Punic Wars. Polybius, a friend of Scipio Aemilianus, who led the Romans against Carthage in the Third Punic War, actually witnessed the destruction of Carthage. This is ancient history come to life, and riveting reading. Highly recommended.

H. H. Scullard, *The Etruscan Cities and Rome*. Ithaca, NY: Cornell University Press, 1967. A scholarly study of the Etruscans and their important contributions to Rome.

————, *Scipio Africanus: Soldier and Politician*. Ithaca, NY: Cornell University Press, 1970. A very scholarly study of the famous Roman general who defeated Hannibal. For serious Roman history buffs only.

Index

Picture Credits

Cover photo: Stock Montage, Inc.

AKG London, 29 (bottom), 45 (bottom), 51

The Bettmann Archive, 11, 12, 32, 38 (top)

Culver Pictures, Inc., 35, 49, 69

Hulton Deutsch, 57

The Mansell Collection, 79, 82

North Wind Picture Archives, 16, 18, 20, 22, 27, 28, 29 (top), 40, 41, 45 (top), 46, 62, 64, 80, 85

Stock Montage, Inc., 19, 38 (bottom), 56, 67, 73, 87

About the Author

Don Nardo is an award-winning author whose more than sixty books cover a wide range of topics, many of them science- and health-related. Titles include *Lasers, Gravity, The Universe, Ozone, Dinosaurs, Eating Disorders, Exercise, Medical Diagnosis,* and *Vitamins and Minerals.* A trained historian and history teacher, Mr. Nardo has produced several historical studies, among them *The War of 1812, The Mexican-American War, Braving the New World, The U.S. Presidency,* and biographies of Thomas Jefferson, Franklin D. Roosevelt, and Joseph Smith. However, his specialty is the ancient world, about which he has written *Ancient Greece, The Roman Republic, The Roman Empire, Traditional Japan, The Battle of Marathon, Greek and Roman Theater, Julius Caesar,* and the companion to this volume on Zama, *The Punic Wars.* In addition, Mr. Nardo has written numerous screenplays and teleplays, including work for Warner Brothers and ABC-Television. He lives with his wife, Christine, on Cape Cod, Massachusetts.